CONTACT

by

AFN CLARKE

40th Anniversary Edition

CLARK*e*- BOOKS

First published in England 1983 by Martin Secker & Warburg Limited 54 Poland Street, London
First paperback edition published in 1984 by PAN Books Ltd. Cavaye Place, London
First American edition published in 1984 by Schocken Books, New York
First expanded eBook edition published in 2012 by Clarke-Books
First expanded softcover edition published in 2014 by Clarke-Books
This 40th Anniversary hardcover edition published 2023 by Clarke-Books

Front cover photograph by Jonathan Olley – www.jonathanolley.com
Cover design by AFN Clarke

ISBN: 978-1-938611-21-6

CLARK*e* - BOOKS

www.afnclarke.com

From reviews of CONTACT

"…the best account we have had of what it is like to serve in Northern Ireland."
Richard West, *Times Literary Supplement*

"…its honesty and passion cannot be denied….Mr Clarke has sent out a powerful and disturbing early warning signal."
Maurice Leitch, *Daily Telegraph*

"…unashamedly personal account…a fascinating view of fighting a war from a perspective which we very rarely experience or hear about."
Michael Keene, *Irish Evening Press*

"…a major contribution to our understanding of war and how people act…*Contact* is the work of a brave writer."
Kevin Toolis, *Irish News*

"…a devastatingly realistic book, as realistic as this morning's headlines…the writing is taut and dramatic…"
Sunday Press, Dublin

"Captain Clarke is more than a serving soldier. He is a writer of distinction."
Jack Gerson, *Glasgow Sunday Standard*

"It is the quality of immediacy which makes *Contact* such an interesting and important book. A present-tense-stream-of-consciousness style has great potential pitfalls - but Clarke brings it off."
David Rose, *Time Out*

"*Contact* is one of the best military stories that I have ever read and I recommend it to you in the highest terms; it's a book from a past conflict that has timely and resonant lessons for a present one."
Steven McLaughlin, author of *Squaddie: A Soldier's Story*

For my Mother

"If peace cannot be maintained with honour it is no longer peace."
Lord John Russell, Sept. 1853

"Necessity is the plea for every infringement of human freedom. It is the argument of tyrants, it is the creed of slaves."
William Pitt, Nov. 1783

CONTENTS

Introduction

This book is written in anger. Anger at previous attempts to portray the British soldier. Anger at the violence and the hatred that became part of a way of life. Anger at the misrepresentation of the facts.

Books about Northern Ireland seem inevitably to turn into political analyses or into novels that stretch credibility to the limit. CONTACT is unashamedly about myself. It is about my own emotions, thoughts and reactions during two tours with the British Army in Northern Ireland. Both tours were with a Regiment both famous and infamous, praised and hated but never ignored: The Parachute Regiment. My Battalion, 3 Para, has had many tours in the province. This book is about two of those tours: one in Belfast in 1973; and the second in Crossmaglen in 1976.

The events described in the book are real. Everything recorded here actually occurred. In order to bring the narrative to life, I have in some cases put words into the mouths of individuals when they were in fact spoken by others. However, the atmosphere, tension, and utter frustration were felt by all. For obvious reasons, certain names have been changed.

If people are offended by this account, that is unfortunate but a necessity. This is about my personal feelings and thoughts, written down in an effort to be brutally honest about the events. Northern Ireland is a catalogue of religious mistakes, political mistakes and military mistakes. It has affected and changed the lives of a large portion of our society. The running tally of the dead continues to grow.

Much has been written about the plight of the Irish people in the battle areas, but a true picture of what goes on behind the eyes that peer through the sights of Army rifles has never emerged. Here are the thoughts and feelings of one soldier, during some of the times of sheer boredom and during the course of incidents that reached the headlines.

A book that tries to be honest is of course open to misinterpretation and to the use of passages out of context to enhance a political argument. This is a risk that must be faced to get at the reality. I abhor, as does any rational being, the use of violence as a political tool, irrespective of who uses it. Nobody realises the waste and sheer stupidity of war more than the British soldier. For it is he who has for centuries had to bear the ordeal of battle, sometimes in opposition to his own feelings. During my seven years in the Parachute Regiment, I met and made friends with many men from widely different backgrounds. I grew to respect them, and to trust most of them with my life.

For the use of strong language I make no apology. These are men talking, soldiers talking. Human beings who are tense and a little afraid for long periods. Few people know of the conditions and the sheer physical hard work; perhaps now they will and on reading of another attack on an Army patrol will think of the following pages, instead of dismissing the incident as yet another episode in a continuing and irrelevant story.

AFN Clarke, 1980.

Author's Note:

I joined the Parachute Regiment as a Private soldier in June 1971 and was commissioned in August the following year, joining 3PARA in Cyprus as part of the United Nations peacekeeping force. The first tour of Northern Ireland began in Belfast in March 1973. On my return I was posted to the Depot in Aldershot as a Recruit Training Officer, returning to 3PARA in 1975. Prior to the second tour in Northern Ireland I served in France, gaining French parachute wings, and with my Company in Norway on NATO exercise. I was recommended for Staff College but had to leave the Army in August 1978 at the end of my contract after several major operations and the loss of my large bowel, the result of complications from the internal bleeding that began during my tour in Crossmaglen, South Armagh in 1976, and that in 1977 the Army medical services failed to address in time, that nearly led to my death. My Army medical records, from the end of 1976 until my discharge in August 1978, mysteriously *'went missing'*. Those medical records would have answered a lot of questions regarding the probability of gross negligence.

Although I wrote about my internal bleeding and surgeries in the first draft manuscript, on the insistence of the publisher - Martin Secker & Warburg – the parts referencing the two months of pain and bleeding during the Crossmaglen tour before I finally had to go to hospital, and my mistreatment by the Army Medical Services were removed. In this new print edition of CONTACT, those parts have been restored and also photographs included that were not in previous editions.

In July 2012, after 35 years fighting the British Government, I was finally awarded a War Disability Pension assessed at 60%. The War Pensions Tribunal that eventually heard the case, having examined all the evidence, concluded that my injury did indeed occur during my

Army service in Northern Ireland, and that the British Army medical services had failed to address the critical nature of my medical condition until it was nearly too late. Sadly my experience is not at all unusual for injured soldiers returning from combat in Afghanistan and Iraq, or anywhere else in the world.

AFN Clarke, 2014

Glossary of Terms

C.O. - Commanding Officer
Company HQ - Company Headquarters
C.S.M. - Company Sergeant-Major
C.Sgt – Colour Sergeant
D.Z. - Drop Zone
G.P.M.G. - General-Purpose Machine Gun
I.W.S. - Individual Weapon Sight
L.S.L. - Troop Ship
L.Z. - Landing Zone
O.C. - Officer Commanding (Company Commander)
OP - Observation Post
Ops Room - Operations Room
P. Check - Personality Check
P.E. - Plastic Explosive
Pig - Armoured Personnel Carrier
Q. Car - Unmarked civilian vehicle used by Army
R.C.T. - Royal Corps of Transport
R.P.G - Handheld Anti-Tank Rocket (Russian made)
R.V. - Rendezvous Point
Saracen - Armoured Personnel Carrier
S.I.B. - Special Investigation Branch
S.L.R. - Self-Loading Rifle
S.M.G. - Sub-Machine Gun
S.O.P - Standard Operating Procedures
S.U.I.T. - Sight Unit Individual Telescopic
TAC HQ. - Tactical Headquarters
Toms - Private Soldiers
2I.C. - Second-in-Command
V.C.P. - Vehicle Checkpoint
X.M.G. - Slang for Crossmaglen

AFN CLARKE

1: Getting Dirty Knees

0400 hrs. April 1973

Cold morning.
Deserted streets.
Rows of terraced houses like calloused fingers stretching out
Through the city.
Silent shadows moving slowly from doorway to doorway.
Tread softly.
"In position now."
Nameless doors, faceless windows.
Silence.
"Go!"

Thirty doors in the Old Park district of Belfast splintered and burst open under the onslaught of Army fury and boots. Over a hundred people turfed out of bed. Screams, yells, thuds, all shatter the morning stillness. The elderly, the infirm, the young, the tired and the lonely.

"Fucking English pigs!"

"Para bastards, youse animals."

"I've got a heart condition, she's got epilepsy."

"Youse broke my door, youse fuckers!"

The abuse is never-ending, the quality never-changing. Now it just rolls off my back and I concentrate on the job. A week ago, one of our section commanders was hit in the stomach by a sniper's bullet, just thirty yards from this house. He was lucky; he managed to get to hospital and the operating theatre. The locals cheered at the time.

The reason for this search was an anonymous telephone call to TAC HQ, possibly placed by one of our own soldiers out for revenge, informing them that there were arms and ammunition hidden somewhere in one of the houses.

The dwellings, one could hardly call them houses, were typical of the ghettos of Belfast, with two rooms upstairs, two down, an outside toilet and an alleyway backing onto the next row, which faced another street. An assortment of sweating humanity lived in sordid conditions of filth, sinks full of greasy plates, cookers black with dirt and spilled, decaying food. Bedrooms with a stench of unwashed bodies and bedclothes, full pots under the beds with the contents liberally sloshed onto the floor. Peeling wallpaper and damp everywhere. Next door, a tidy house. An elderly couple, well used to early morning searches, are quietly resigned. Aggressive soldiers are suddenly calmed; one uses the old man's tools to patch up the broken door. The screams of abuse don't enter here. The old lady makes tea in the scullery while the old man talks of the old days. As the search team leaves, a gentle touch on the arm:

"Be careful, son, there's some bad people in this street."

"Tell us who, Dad."

The face closes and the brief contact is broken.

Further down the street a middle-aged woman is throwing a fit in the middle of her front room. Nightdress up over her hips. Pale fat legs flailing around, breasts flopping out of the nightie's flimsy material. The soldiers standing around hooting with laughter.

"Come on you old cow, show us what you've got."

"Hey, Smiffy, how'd you like to get up that?"

"O.K. lads, just watch your stations. Let her get on with it. If you get a hard-on over that Jones, there's something wrong with you."

There's a series of catcalls and laughter. Without an audience the woman picks herself up and sits down on the settee. An impression nags in my mind of a shadow flitting down an alley. Just a feeling. The search teams move from house to house, slowly, methodically opening every door, pulling out every drawer and spreading the contents of human existence over the floor. Private lives pried into, private weaknesses revealed, private wounds exposed, all laid open to the eager eyes and ears of a degraded society.

The soldiers on the street shift position constantly. Eyes scanning rooftops and windows, not letting a single person out of the cordon, and not letting a single person in.

"Over here, boss."

The call for a P. Check.

"O.K. Paddy, hands against the wall. Feet spread. Name. Address. Age."

The list is endless and repeated hundreds of times a day.

Experience has taught me to have my own 'heavy' with me during on the street questioning, any negative replies warrant a thump, threatening behaviour an immediate arrest and trip to TAC HQ before release or further treatment at Castlereagh.

The hate is in the eyes, but the banners are gone and nobody on their own airs their feelings any more. The search has been on for four hours now, and it's raining, which doesn't bother us, of course, we're Paras. Rain, snow, sunshine, it's all the same; or so they say. Rain dripping from the ends of noses, running down gun barrels. Feet sore from standing. In the distance, a plume of smoke rises in the city centre followed an instant later by the dull boom of an explosion. Faces lift up for a brief moment.

"Car bomb," grunts my Sergeant, more for something to say than to divulge valuable information. The Toms move around restlessly.

Inside one of the houses the search team has encountered a bit of aggro. The commotion stirs the pot once more. Bottles appear from over the rooftops and splinter over the road. One Tom slips on the wet surface diving for cover and sprawls with a clatter on the ground.

"You two with me. John, take another couple round the other way."

We sprint round the corner, dodging the hail of bottles and rocks.

"Get that dick gun up here." Pause. "Right, zap that little cunt."

A loud report and the rubber bullet thwacks into a teenage boy, catching him between the legs. A Corporal and his patrol appear from a door and, more by luck than planning, fall onto the unfortunate boy and drag him back to a waiting Pig. It's over before it's started. The remainder of the mob fragmented and dispersed amongst the houses.

Anxious faces peer more keenly at rooftops and windows, street corners and doorways. The tactics have always been to precede a sniper attack with a riot of some description. On a few rifles, safety catches are thumbed off, the butt pulled more firmly into the shoulder and our eyes try to see into every nook and cranny.

"Hookey, take a patrol round the perimeter."

My platoon sergeant selects his men, and quietly moves away in the rain, the last men in the patrol walking backwards. As they move further away they take on the appearance of American footballers. Flak jackets underneath smocks give the impression that a small weedy person is suddenly gifted with a Tarzan-like physique. The bulk is purposeful. Intimidate by appearance.

The morning drifts on. Six hours into the search and nothing found. Just one more to add to the growing list of nothing. The earphone crackles, and the welcome signal to move passes down to the section commanders. The high whine of the Saracens splits the air as they grind slowly off up the street. Rifle barrels pointing out through open rear doors. Expressionless faces peering all round. We steadily patrol back to our own area, having been drafted in for this search. Rain-covered streets and alleys, soaked soldiers. All communication by sign language, a unique way of talking. A complete compendium of phrases in nods and winks, arm waves and rifle movements. Home is a disused police station. Home is hot food and a hot drink. Home is to get your head down because we're out in two hours for an area foot patrol.

Sandbagged entrance with helmeted sentry. Clear all weapons. The procedure has become second nature now. Patrol report. Debrief the patrol. Anyone see anything? Usual negative reply.

"O.K., get into your maggots and crash. Tom, yours is the next patrol. In two days we start OPs." Sighs of relief. The only time the section commanders have to get some rest. Patrol report filed in the Ops room. Usual banter with the duty officer, flop into a chair and flake out.

The O.C. is doing his trick, falling asleep in the middle of writing out the following week's patrol programme. The C.S.M. is playing with the new Company toy - a videotape machine. The radio operator is answering the routine calls on the set as well as listening to the other traffic and concentrating on the unusual antics of a couple in one of Denmark's best porno magazines. Well, life is normal after all.

The crick in my neck wakes me up. The O.C. is asleep again or at least in the process of. The C.S.M. has set up the video camera and is carefully placing a pencil under the O.C.'s chin. Gentle snores, slowly descending chin and - *voilà*! The perfect balancing act. The only sound for the next few minutes is the quiet whirring of the video.

Last week it was my section commander, putting more pressure on the already fractured brain of the Battalion Commanding Officer, by doing his Harvey the invisible six-foot white rabbit routine. The C.O. was actually trying to shake hands with this myth. A few days later, he was posted. The C.O., that is. Paul and Harvey were still alive and well and freaking the locals. No way to get any peace here.

I wander through the dim interior of Leopold Street police station. Dark interiors of rooms. Pale faces staring out unseeing, rifles at the ready, fully clothed. Confused minds still half asleep. Somewhere in the background a tinny tape machine whines out the thin beat of a bad song.

Into the bright neon-lit canteen, Mohammed, our pet Paki, lurks behind his counter waiting to relieve the Toms of their money in return for cigarettes, Pepsi, hot dogs, etc. Never once in the entire five months of the tour did I see him poke his head out of his hole. With all the money he made I should think he is now set up in a nice business driving a Rolls around. One half-can of beer. Seal the cracks in your brain with that.

The T.V. sits accusingly behind its wire cage. The Toms flopped around in chairs too tired to talk. Desultory conversation drifts around the lower part of the anatomy. Fantasies of mounds of naked female flesh. Worldly-wise at eighteen. Cram it all in, some of you don't have too much time.

Somehow I found my way upstairs and into the Sgts. and Officers Mess. Well, one room where we can sit and be disloyal, traitorous, hatch mutinies without anyone being any the wiser. Then carry on with the job. Job? What job? It becomes a way of life. A way to continue existing from one day to the next.

"Lt. Clarke, are you up there?" A bellow from the intercom.

"Yeah!"

"O.C. wants you."

"O.K."

What now? Another patrol. Search. An OP. Weary feet dragging downstairs. Tired brain shaking awake. Apparently there is a suspected bomb in a house a couple of streets away and I have to investigate. Great! Just what I need to blow the cobwebs away. Shit, these things scare the fuck out of me.

"O.K. fellas, we're just going to stroll over and have a look at a house just around the corner. Some guy says there's a bomb in it." Cheers from the section, happiness written all over their scowling faces.

"I notice you haven't volunteered, Hookey!"

My platoon sergeant just shakes his head with a wry smile. "My name's Hunt not Cunt."

Casually walking down the street, chewing gum, trying to look hard and unconcerned, heart pounding like a steam hammer gone mad, palms sweaty, and a huge claw tearing away in the pit of my stomach.

It's just another scare... They are trying to set us up... It's a booby trap... There's a hidden sniper. It's for real this time... All the possibilities ping round my brain. Holy fuck, why not call in the bomb blokes?

The street looks just as always. Drab terraced housing sloshed with rain. Half a dozen in a derelict condition, the others empty, a few at either end inhabited. Stall for time.

"Hello 3, this is 33 Alpha, say again number of house, over."

"3 wait out." Pause.

"Hello 33 Alpha, this is 3. Number is 21, over."

"33 Alpha, Roger out."

Come on, Clarke, get your finger out, if you're going to go, there is not an awful lot you can do about it. Twenty-one is just across the street. Position a Tom on each corner and take one with me. Hell, why die alone.

In through the upstairs window, I think. Climb on a willing back. I collapse through the window and sit there shaking like a leaf. The whole room is littered with old clothes, newspapers, shit, and God knows what else. Just look for any pressure pads, trip-wires or pull switches. Top floor search over. Nothing. Move to the top of the stairs. There could be a pressure pad on any one of those steps. We look around for something heavy. A piece of wardrobe, that will do. It clatters down the stairs and lies at the bottom looking at me.

"You O.K. boss?"

"Yeah." I join it at the bottom of the stairs.

Twenty minutes later I'm standing on the street, enjoying the cool rain splashing on my face.

"Right, guys, just another rubber dick. Let's go." One day one of these tips is going to be real. I just don't want to be around when it is. Right now, I'm just very relieved.

Back to Leopold Street and up the stairs. I must have some sleep if only for an hour or two. The average for the past week has been two hours in twenty-four. The mileage per day does not bear thinking about. Flop onto the bed. I've only been between the sheets three times in the month the tour has been going. Some time a change of clothes would be very welcome.

It's daylight outside, but in here with the light off it's dark. A pale grey light struggling through the black-painted window. All the windows in the place are painted out and the Ops Room is encased in two-foot-thick concrete with a further layer of sandbags on the outside.

Clive, one of my fellow platoon commanders, shares this room with me but I haven't seen him for a week as he has been on one of the OPs. Next week my platoon will be on the OPs so after a brief handover, we won't see each other for a further week. Are we in the same Army?

I drift off to sleep amidst the sweet sound of a Saracen whining off down the road on another patrol, and the distant rumbling thud of another car bomb in the city centre.

"Sir, O.C. wants you." I struggle awake; who is this apparition thumping me and bellowing in my ear?

"O.C. sir, wants you right away." Fuck the O.C., fuck the Irish, fuck the Army.

"O.K. Green, don't shout for Christ's sake. Hey, get a brew on and bring it into the Ops Room, will you."

"Can't sir, just going on patrol."

"Then tell some other cunt."

The O.C. is O.K.; he just nods off to sleep in mid-sentence. We figured he managed to get at least a full eight hours just by dropping off at his desk. He didn't need a bed to sleep on. Yesterday, he even fell out of his Landrover. Lucky for him, the driver still hadn't learnt where the accelerator was otherwise it would have been nasty. As it was, he just picked himself up, shook his head and climbed back in. He even fell asleep whilst briefing us on back-up patrol after a contact in the Ardoyne. Now everyone just takes it in their stride and Brian delights in taking videos of him asleep.

I move zombie-like, downstairs again - think I'll move my bed into the Ops Room. At the bottom there is a violent commotion. Brian has apparently caught a sentry asleep in one of the base OPs and is busy kicking him all around the stand-by room. His anger was further inflamed when he tried to hit the poor unfortunate, who ducked, and Brian broke his hand on the offered steel helmet.

"Stupid fucking cow." Thud, kick. "Asshole," etc., etc.

There is no formal charging of offenders in this Company. The treatment may be rough but it is short and effective. We can't afford to have anybody languishing in the cells. There is not enough manpower as it is.

The O.C. looks up bleary-eyed as I enter. He's just woken up and even recognition is difficult at this moment.

"Tony, another patrol please. Some disturbance on the Shankill down by Agnes Street. There is a patrol there at the moment but I want to block off the top end of the Crumlin with a V.C.P., and have another V.C.P. at this end near the Woodvale Road, Ballygomartin Road junction."

"Where do you want me?"

"On the Woodvale, Peter will put his on the Crumlin." I motion to Paul, one of my section commanders, and he goes out to round up the lads.

V.C.P.s give us the chance to fly around in stripped-down Landrovers and when I say stripped-down, I mean stripped-down. No doors, no roof, no tailgate, no windshield. It means we can bail out in seconds in a contact situation, and whilst driving, have maximum vision. On days like today, with the rain, we would all prefer a cosy Saracen or Pig.

Out into the cold wet April afternoon. Where the hell did lunch go? The Landrovers are bristling with rifles - four men in the back of each, facing outwards. The driver and one in the front. We drive slowly amongst the Belfast traffic. No cars pass. The locals have been warned to stay clear of any Army vehicles. At night, oncoming or following vehicles douse their lights. If they don't, they are stopped, searched and on occasions have had their lights smashed. Up near our destination we swing the vehicles across the road, blocking both lanes. Rear four out into fire positions, driver down by the vehicle, leaving myself and the platoon sergeant in the middle. He has the search team in his vehicle. We stop all the cars and back the traffic up the road. Then take the numbers of cars turning around at the sight of the V.C.P. and relay to a mobile patrol.

"Would you please step out of your car and open the bonnet and boot." It takes time to go through each car and P. Check the occupants. O.K., move off. Occasionally we get abuse but mostly people are well used to this sort of thing. We even got two Royal Navy clowns in this V.C.P. out for a sightseeing tour of the city. Didn't someone tell them that they could get killed doing that sort of thing? Jesus! Sit in their boats month after month and then think they might see a bit of action to tell their mates about. Here mate, swop places with me!

Ten minutes the V.C.P. has been on. I start to get jumpy standing around for too long. Just make sure that there are lots of cars and people standing around to spoil the chances of a sniper. Trouble is, being a placed V.C.P. we cannot lift it at our own discretion and have to wait for orders. Please don't go to sleep, Major. Not this time.

There is a commotion behind us and one of the Toms emerges

from a bush with a scruffy young teenager in tow.

"Found him hiding in the house behind us, sir. Keep still you little shit or I'll pan you!"

Lay him face down on the road and P. Check. He must be up to something because he is just not at all nervous. Very unsettling that. Still, one consolation is that he is not very good at whatever he was up to. Perhaps he was trying to pick up some Brownie points with the local U.V.F., or Tartan gang. He clears out on the P. Check but we can still lift him on suspicion. Keep him on the deck until this V.C.P. is over. He's quiet enough at the moment.

The cars keep coming through, but it's a slow process. Wet beret clamped to my head, denims clinging to my legs, it is difficult to move around, talk into the radio and write down car numbers at the same time. The harsh sound of the ghetto Irish grinds in my ears. Girls look good until they open their mouths and a stream of expletives rolls easily off their pretty little tongues.

Fifteen minutes. Come on, Major.

Nervous eyes flicker up to the Holy Cross church just up the road a bit. The last Battalion on this area were sniped at from the tower a few times, and last year some guy was blown up by a booby trap in the graveyard. An Irish terrorist with a sense of humour yet! Rain still bucketing down; at least these others are getting soaked too.

"Any mouthy buggers, keep them out in the rain longer, Hookey."

"O.K. boss."

It's easy to get mean when you are holding the trump cards, isn't it, Clarke. Shit, why not? We don't get any favours from them and anyway, most of these buggers would shoot me in the back as soon as look at me. So? Fuck, forget it. The radio crackles, good old Major, not asleep after all. Hookey hears it as well and in two minutes we are halfway back to Leopold Street.

Sitting here in the de-briefing room, I'm having difficulty in believing I'm not in dreamland. Telephones are appearing from thin air. Black ones, blue ones, red, yellow. Normal types, fancy ones, thin, fat.

"What's this with the telephones then?"

"I need an extension at home," pause, "and one in the bedroom, one in the toilet, one in the garage..." it goes on and on.

"O.K., O.K., but how?"

"Just asked the telephone engineer in the van we stopped. Nervous type, you know."

Jesus, what next. Three-piece suites, refrigerators? As it happens, yes. All manner of goodies were being salted away in secret places to be shipped back to England at the end of the tour, as part of the platoon freight. Some freight. Still, back in England, our platoon office was very well equipped. My spare telephone never worked, though.

"Right, forget the telephones, de-brief. Anyone have anything to say?" Series of shaking heads.

"Yeah, boss, that little shit who was spying on us."

Of course, I had forgotten about him. He was, in fact, at that moment being interrogated by our own Company Int. cell. We preferred to try for some information before the ham-fisted twits at TAC HQ got hold of them. Usually they let them go because the idiot we had as Intelligence Officer thought that all the energy should be expended in the direction of the Ardoyne. We were later to leave him and the rest of the Battalion with egg on their faces, as at the end of the day we had the most finds and kills to our credit. So up yours, I.O.

De-briefing over, pasty faces and tired bodies make their way to find a brew and food. Hookey and I sit alone, staring at the mound of telephones.

"You've got to have a go at the O.C., boss. We can't carry on at this pace forever. The blokes are beginning to crack."

"How about giving each Tom a day off? We can fill in with one of the cooks or the R.C.T. drivers. On their day off, they can get pissed, sleep, or do what they like. It's not much, but it may just ease the pressure."

"Not a bad idea."

So the day-off system was born. The only ones that did not get time off were the section commanders, Hookey and myself. The problems of being in command.

I look in at the Ops Room on the way through to get a much-needed bite to eat. I swear the O.C. hasn't moved from the spot for the last forty-eight hours straight. The 2I.C. sits staring at the map humming tunelessly. His main objective in life at the moment is to get through this tour without ever having to put his head outside the door. The radio op. still has that same magazine.

"Two's up."

"On your bike, sir!"

The O.C. hands me the next week's programme and I see that he has decided that the OP platoon does very little during the week, so now they will have to do some patrolling around the immediate area. Just the sort of thing to raise morale to another all-time high. Well, what else do we have to do? Did someone mention overtime? What's that?

"Our area is going to be extended to include the entire Forthriver area. We take over next month."

Oh, delight. Much cheering. Can we go home now! That means that we will now have an area four times the size of the Ardoyne with half the number of men to cover it. What lunatic in the Northern Ireland Office dreams these amazing things up? Some civil servant sitting at a desk playing with figures on a piece of paper.

"Just going to take this guy we brought in over to TAC HQ and hand him over to Int. See what sort of a mess they are into up there." Anything to get out, before I throw a fit and hurl my rifle across the room.

TAC HQ, that veritable fountain of all knowledge. Housed in the main police station in Tennant Street, it is supposed to be the nerve centre of the Battalion. The C.O. and remainder of Battalion hierarchy live in their own little dream world surrounded by radios, maps, files and God knows what else tucked away in drawers and locked steel cupboards.

The Int. section is, as usual, empty. Until a beautifully turned out corporal comes in, turns his nose up at our dishevelled appearance, and very condescendingly asks us what we want. We hand over the scruffy urchin. Then check on one of my men doing guard duty and go outside to wait the ten minutes it usually takes TAC to release anyone we bring in. Here he is. Grab the urchin again and give him the gypsy's warning.

"Once more mate and you're for the high dive. Just show your face near a patrol again. Now, fuck off."

An angry bee buzzes past my ear, and another one. That is no bee, that's a low-velocity round. The Winchester Street cowboy.

"Contact, wait, out."

Heart pounding. Legs refusing to run properly. Ham-fisted cocking the rifle.

Dive into doorways... cover the next guy... sprint again.

When we arrive, there's nothing. Empty street beckoning. Curious passers-by stare. Two empty cases lying on the ground. Check the immediate house. Crash straight through the doors and race upstairs. No sign. Check the alleys. Nothing. By the time the stand-by section has arrived everything has cooled off. One day, we'll get that bastard. He's been pestering us for weeks. Two rounds and he's off and running. But where to? Still, so far he hasn't hurt anyone so he can't be that good a shot.

The next hour is taken up with a search through the immediate area. We finish in the dark in both senses of the word. So a routine delivery of a prisoner to TAC HQ ends up with an hour-and-a-half search. That leaves time to get back to Leopold Street, get the lads fed and ready for their official patrol in an hour's time. Think I'll shy off that one. Why not, I'm out on the Ardoyne back-up patrol at midnight, plus the admin that needs to be done to sort out the organisation for the week coming up.

Leopold Street, sweet Leopold Street.

We clear the weapons and go through the patrol report procedure again. This time happy in the knowledge that at least now there is something to put down on that forbidding blank piece of paper.

Catcalls and chorus of "Useless" and "Couldn't catch a cold." Boring. The cook is doing us proud, and like all artists is throwing a tantrum at the irregularity of the hours we keep and "How can I possibly turn out cooked meals twenty-four hours a day?" I don't know how he does it, but the food is always good and always hot.

Tea, that elixir of life. Saviour of the British Empire. Hot, in huge, black, plastic cups. After the excitement of the last hour, the section flop into the chairs in the cookhouse and quietly eat their meal. Some drift off to finish letters, others to make phone calls home. Some to lie down, others to continue the weeks-long arguments as to which football team is the best in England. Me, I'm upstairs in the Mess staring at the T.V. without actually seeing it.

Brian's cursing over some admin hiccup in the otherwise perfect running of the Company. Hookey, like me, is collapsed in a chair, snoring. My eyes now closing. Tiredness creeping over me. Drifting into half sleep...

Tired and wet! I've been here before! Strange thoughts. Half unconscious flashback images stealing around the murky corridors of my mind. Half back in Belfast, the other here in cold wet Brecon.

"Come on! Get up! Move your ass." I'm yelling at a mud-and-rain-soaked recruit, trying to haul himself off the ground.

"Get that fucking rifle barrel out of the mud, you stupid shit." All this above the crack of S.L.R.s and the shouts of my N.C.O.s at the rest of the section. The ground is uneven clods of thick grass, hidden holes and pools of water. Ahead a fifteen-foot-wide stream. There's a gasp as the crow in front of me hits the ice-cold water and wallows around up to his chest, weighted down by thirty pounds of equipment.

"Come on you fairy this isn't a swimming pool! Get across!" It's the second time I've been across the stream, so I'm already soaked through and freezing cold. There's a certain delight in watching somebody else do it. To the right an ashen faced crow lying on the ground, his rifle moving in a lazy arc.

"Smith, you bastard, you're supposed to be covering. Get

that rifle firing." He looks at me and for a brief second thinks of unloading the entire magazine of live rounds into my chest. The N.C.O. behind hits him with a large lump of wood and amid screams of abuse, Smith hauls himself off the ground and wades through the water.

Despite all the abuse the lads are working well, moving carefully but quickly and, apart from the occasional desire to give up, getting on with the job in hand. The "job" is to capture a sniper position up on the hill in front of us, the position being "held" by wooden targets. The back brace on one target is shot through and starts to topple. Before it hits the ground a burst from the machine gun, over on the right flank, smashes it to tiny pieces. Jones, the crow in front of me, zigzags forwards while Smith covers him. Smith is approaching exhaustion and starting to give up. He fires, and the round smacks into the ground inches away from Jones' left boot, whines away over the hill.

"Smith you little shit, what the fuck are you trying to do?" He looks a little shaken. "Bill, sort that cunt out," I shout to Cpl. Conway. Just one more incident to talk about once the exercise is over.

The rain is coming down harder now, the icy drops lancing into my face, stinging; sodden beret clamped to head, smock twice its weight with water. This is the most dangerous part of the exercise. Tired crows nearing the end, bunching together, firing at the targets now only twenty-five metres ahead.

"Apply safety catches and skirmish through the objective." I try and counter the noise. The N.C.O.s catch the call and the firing ceases. Euphoria that they have reached the objective takes over and the crows skirmish through, screaming and cursing. I hand over to Cpl. Conway, who carries on with the reorganisation and consolidation of the position, and walk over to a small outcrop of rock at the top of the hill. Looking back across the valley to a small wood

about two hundred metres away, three figures emerge and start running with the awkward gait of men laden down with heavy equipment. Every so often one of them trips and stumbles over the rough ground, but they keep on coming. As they get closer I can hear the rasping pants as they struggle for air, their kit clunking and squelching, bruising their hips.

L.Cpl. Hedges brings the gun crew in on my signal and positions them. I feel good.

The sound of singing and splashing carries up through the valley and figures appear at the door of the hut to watch the procession. Standing out in the pouring rain, cold and wet with huge smiles on their faces, shouting obscenities together with derisive gestures. Four months ago, they were just a bunch of out-of-work unfit youths who fancied themselves as paratroopers. Out of the seventy that originally formed the platoon, there are thirty here on the range. And they are all fit, healthy and happy. Sometimes.

Time to stop the daydream and get the last section through. So it's trot down the hill, wade through the stream and nonchalantly stroll up to where the section is waiting. Fully kitted out. Laden down with ammunition and other equipment. Now slightly nervous, as the moment of truth has finally arrived.

"O.K. lads. Listen in. Safety procedures..." I run through the briefing, give them the scenario and off we go again. My platoon Sgt. just grins and disappears back inside the hut, muttering something about having to get on with the admin. His words echo strangely in the doorway.

"The Ardoyne was..."

"Ardoyne..." Someone in the background talking. Waking me.

The word is emotive enough in Army circles. That such a small area could cause so much suffering and hardship is barely credible. Before we arrived in the place, no police had been into the area, no taxes had been paid, rates, electricity bills, nothing. How big? It was split into two. The old Ardoyne and the new. The old is about three hundred yards long by the same width, crowded with terraced housing. The new is slightly bigger with a more modern standard of terraced housing. Surrounded by OPs, five in all, with nearly two hundred and fifty men patrolling it by day and night. Still the shootings occurred. Ambushes, bombs thrown. Delightful little spot to spend four or five months of your life.

Awake again. Mouth like the inside of a fisherman's boot. Numb joints, numb mind. Toms standing in the dull glow of the light bulb. Rifles in hand, slings attached to wrists. Blackened badges on battered berets. Listless shuffling, mindless banter. I file the planned route in the Ops Room and then we go out into the clammy cold midnight air. It's stopped raining. Score one against Sod's Law. Cover across the Crumlin Road. Slippery street and few cars. Up by Fort Knox and slip quietly and unobtrusively into the Ardoyne.

The street is deserted, flanked by black shadows. Rooftops in relief against the night sky. The quiet crackle of static in my earphone, whispered reply, distant acknowledgement. Eyes and ears wide open, trying to penetrate inky darkness, decipher sounds, interpret shapes.

We stop at a crossroads. Rifle down at side, peer carefully round the corner. Same on the other side. Signal across. Two-hundred-pound soldier skips quickly and quietly across the street and disappears into a shadow. Next across, and the next. All now safe in new street. The other section appears as planned, on other corner. We vanish down a parallel street keeping in touch.

Whitewashed walls and then sudden light. Duck, and crouch in a doorway. Scan the upper windows. Approaching the Brompton Gap. It's dangerous here but not tonight. Slip into the Brompton Alley. Paul's patrol is still parallel with us. Send two men down to the end. Cover them down. O.K., move. Slowly down the alley. Nameless doors on faceless houses. A child crying in the night. Ignored. There's a noise at the bottom of the street, two drunks weaving unsteadily in the direction of the stagger. We quietly appear from nowhere and watch the fright in their eyes. The quickest way to sober up. P.

Check. Nothing.

There's a crackle in the earphone from OP on the top of the Flax Street Mill. Apparently, there's a fight two streets across. Looks like someone trying to cleave another's head open. When we arrive, cautiously, moving slowly, not trusting the situation, we find two brothers in the process of hammering the hell out of each other. Two wives are screaming. We separate them and give each a crack over the head with a truncheon. P. Check. Nothing. They all go off to their own houses massaging sore heads. We resume our patrol and wander round the area in seeming abandon, carefully planned with no pattern. Our rubber-soled boots make no noise, just the occasional cough or suppressed sneeze. Clink of metal against brick. Quiet night. Thank God.

There have been two ambushes in this street alone during the past week. No casualties. Just one Tom with a hole through his notebook and a slight graze on the inside of his thigh where the bullet had passed, but one of our night patrols had spotted a sniper coming out of his house with an Armalite. He was hit once in the head and was dead before reaching the ground. Paras 1, I.R.A. 0.

A dull thud, again from the city centre. It has been a day for car bombs. Three already. Now we take no notice. It becomes part of our lives.

"What happened yesterday?"

"Nothing much. House searches, suspected bomb, Winchester Street cowboy at it again. Snap V.C.P.s and more bombs in the city centre. How about you?"

"Oh, dead boring really. Helped B. Company out with a search. Bit of aggro, nothing much. Found a few rounds and a pistol. O.C. fell out of his Landrover again."

0900 hrs. May 1973

Sandbagged security.
Lonely vigil.
Timeless action through sightless slit.
Sleep.
Watch.
Sleep.
Eat.
Sleep.
Watch.

Hookey's in Fort Cross. I'm in Fort Knox. How come he's got the best one twice in a row? The platoon is now on OPs. The two this company has to look after are both on the Crumlin Road, both looking into the Ardoyne. In each Fort, there are two positions to man, connected to the control desk via the intercom system with a radio back-up. Each position has a pair of binoculars, panoramic photograph of the area with reference points marked, and the all-powerful image intensifying sight. In Fort Cross, there is also an intruder alarm system based on infrared and connected to the control desk. It has also been the cause of many a heart-stopping moment.

Fort Cross is an old house at the end of a derelict row of bombed-out and fire-gutted houses, right on the so-called peace line. That line of corrugated tin separating two communities. The Holy Cross church looms over the Fort, and constant clearance patrols are required to check out the graveyard for sniper positions, weapons caches, booby traps and whatever else our Irish friends have devised to entertain us. Inside it is falling apart, and the stairs up to the attic are dangerous, but the attic must be checked every day because there is a mouse-hole that runs the entire length of the block of terracing, all of which are derelict. Although it is blocked with barbed wire there is nothing to prevent a determined bomber slipping through one night and catching us. We put our own little nasty surprises up in the attic of the next-door house. A booby trap of our own, made out of "acquired" P.E. And dismantled by us after each tour of duty and before handing over to the next platoon.

Fort Knox is based upon what used to be the toilets of a pub that was destroyed during the sectarian violence of a few years ago. Stuck in the middle of a piece of waste ground, it is the most vulnerable to attack. The object of the two Forts is to cover patrols moving around in the area and to keep a constant eye on the population. A log is kept of every movement, every radio message, any suspicion, anything.

Clive cheerfully hands over. I've never seen him look anything but happy. With a crazy sense of humour and a complete disregard for danger, he provides a constant stream of anecdotes, jokes and warmth. The Toms still talk about his drunken escapade on top of the roof of a four-ton truck in Cyprus, careering down a mountainside at breakneck speed.

"You will be pleased to know that they are going to do some maintenance on the main sewerage drain that runs under the floor. Stag on!"

And with that, disappears off to Leopold Street and two weeks of patrols. The sentries are briefed and up in the OPs, the rest sacked out. The two Corporals are arguing about who is going to do the cooking. Within five minutes of taking over, normal routine is established.

The argument settled, Jimmy flops onto his bed, Paul gets a brew on and I sit and stare at the wall map listening to the radio traffic of P. Checks, car checks, coded messages of patrol locations and the occasional whispered message from a covert OP.

This tiny desk mounted on duckboards and surrounded by sandbags will be my entire world between eighteen and twenty hours a day for the next week. It's the only way the N.C.O.s are able to recharge their depleted energy store and stay sane. Belfast is an N.C.O.s war, and there are only three per platoon, excluding the platoon sergeant. Paul is cursing in the excuse for a kitchen. It used to be the men's urinal, and still has the same look to it.

"No fucking butter. No fucking meat. Just enough tea for a few brews, but no fresh milk. When's the resup due, boss?"

"This afternoon. The cook's coming across in the Pig."

"Do you want a bacon sarney, boss? There's a bit of bread."

"Yeah. Cheers."

Eat. Read. Listen to the radio. Check the OPs are still awake.

"OP 1. Everything O.K.?"

"Yeah."

"OP 2. Everything O.K.?"

"Yeah."

Later on I'll take a walk up to the positions. Break the routine, see if they are awake and concentrating. Day stretches on interminably, broken by the changing of stags, tea and food. Dirty magazines by the dozen are stacked on the floor. Most left there after the first glance. A pile of sad fantasies gathering dust, most of the best pages have been ripped out and now adorn the walls, and go un-noticed except by newcomers. Sightless eyes stare at oversize nipples, spread thighs, beckoning tongue, dreaming of the girl at home. Home, a long way off. When was I there last? A two-month-old baby that I have only seen for a brief few minutes before departing for the boat. Last impression of my wife still doped after childbirth unable to comprehend my farewell. Harry, one of the Toms, talking quietly in my ear. Me not listening.

"Sorry, mate, what was that? I was away with the fairies."

"Just want to have a word with you about a private matter. You're a married man so you understand these things. It's my wife. You see, she doesn't seem to be able to have an orgasm when we make love, and I don't know what to do about it."

At first I thought he was having me on. Good God, since when have I been an authority on the female orgasm? Women are just as much a mystery to me as the moon.

"That's nothing unusual," says I, "lots of women have difficulty with orgasms." Sound knowledgeable. You can't have an N.C.O. with less than 100% of his mind on the job at hand. "Just needs a bit of experimentation, that's all." We sat talking for an hour or so, with me treading as though through a minefield. He went away happier and fell asleep on his bunk. The radio crackles.

"Hello 33, this is 3 Alpha. Open door, over."

"33 Wilco out."

Buzz.

"OP 1?"

"There's a Pig on its way, keep a look out. It's going to be outside for some time unloading goodies."

"O.K. boss."

The rations have arrived. Joy and jubilation.

"O.K., let's have a couple of you guys out here for the rations." Groans. Creaking of springs. Tousled heads. Red-rimmed eyes. Cam-cream covered faces. Why did you join the Army, son?

Geordies, Welsh, Brummies, Scots and others all go to make up the Company casserole, dished up to each platoon to be garnished with a collective identity yet preserving their individual flavour. Nine platoon. My platoon. Dear God, let us all get back in one piece.

Time now in the Fort to sit and reflect upon the characters as if seeing them for the first time. Patrols leave no time to see each person as they are, beneath the false bravado. The affected crudeness. In some the violence is real and vicious, in others it has been acquired as part of a survival kit. The weak are protected from others outside the platoon, and yet are mercilessly hounded from within. The oldest soldier is twenty and at twenty-five I'm considered an old man.

With the rations comes the work party to fix the sewerage drain under the floor. Complete with pneumatic drills, picks and other assorted tools. Jesus, what the hell are they going to do here? It didn't take long to find out. They moved the bunks out of the way and started drilling a channel across from one corner of the sleeping area to the other, exposing an offshoot of the main drain.

The stench of shit drifted up and hung in the Fort like a cloud, only to get worse the further the workmen drilled. It was difficult to believe it was real, but it was just accepted like everything else in this whole goddam mess. Freaky images of Toms fast asleep whilst a turd floats past. Others eating greasy meals in the fug of an unventilated room.

Eighteen hours is a long time, and my head is doing strange things on my shoulders. Eyeballs feeling like sand-covered marbles. My throat is dry from cigarettes. Nicotine-stained fingers drawing matchstick men on bits of paper. I hang a radio round my neck and check the OPs.

OP 1 looks out into the Ardoyne down two streets, with a further view rearwards towards the Crumlin. The platoon mascot, with a stutter and a permanent stoop, is on duty.

"See anything."

"N-N-N-Nothing, s-s-sir."

"O.K., just keep your eyes open." Where do we get these guys? How do they appear to outsiders? Hard? Cruel? Experienced? Or do others see them as I do? Kids. Just young kids.

OP 2 takes a bit of getting to. It is separated from the rest of the Fort by an alley of corrugated tin about fifteen yards long. The idea is to sprint to the ladder leading up to the position, leap up to it and hope the guy in the OP has unlocked the door by the time you get there. The incidence of low-velocity rounds being fired at slow-moving sentries is enough to keep you on your toes. Once inside you're safe enough, even from a rocket attack, but there is nowhere to go. On stag in this one is a cockney with an accent as big as Tower Bridge:

"Cor, fuckin' 'ell, sir, when's me fuckin' stag finish?"

"Watch your arcs, Renwick, I'll tell you when."

"Make sure fuckin' Smiffy's not late, will you, sir?"

"Keep your voice down."

The grumbling continues in a lower tone. We try and keep the OPs looking like silent, menacing sentinels, so noise must be kept to a minimum.

Through the slit I can see a Support Company patrol moving from doorway to doorway, street to street. Rear two men now totally used to walking backwards. Seeming to know exactly when to go and when to stop. The link established with the other patrol members through long hours of practice, and many miles of Irish tarmac.

Flax Street Mill looms away to the right with their OPs right on top, hidden from the view of anyone on the street. Below the real OP is the false one with mechanical sentries moving around inside. The idea being to lure a gunman with the dummy, and then zap him with the real one. So far it has worked twice, with one kill. The first time our sniper missed the gunman, but made sure the second time around with a perfect shot in the centre of the target. Everyone cheered, of course. It's not until a long time afterwards that the full impact of death comes home to you, but at the time it's a thing of enjoyment and morale soars. Paras 2, I.R.A. 0.

"Look, sir!"

Renwick jars me back from my musings. Some little kids are following the Support Company patrol, the youngest barely four years old. As they walk, they pick up stones and throw them at the patrol, hurling abuse at the same time. The "yellow card" doesn't tell you what to do with little kids, although they have been used time and again as cover for gunmen. The patrol moves slowly on its way, ignoring them. At first it was difficult to believe that small children could have that hate; now, anything is possible and the values we came over with are lying broken with the bottles and shattered brickwork. Women come out of doorways to yell and scream as the men are lined up and searched.

Impassive faces scan the skyline. Impervious eyes watch.

Back in the Fort, at the control desk, I'm trying to write a letter home. It's not easy. To survive you have to suppress all emotion, so writing home becomes a catalogue of platitudes, anything you think they might like to hear.

Jimmy's woken up and brings another brew, then sits reading a Forum magazine; bored, he tosses it down to join the pile gathering dust and takes out a Western book. Next month he's off to do a platoon sergeant's course at Brecon, which is a pity, I really need him on the streets; he's the best section commander I've got.

There's an enormous explosion. We are shaken off our seats. Jimmy's the first to his feet and I follow him through the dust and stink of explosive to the OP. The door is still locked.

"Tully, you O.K?"

A mumble from inside. The door opens and a dazed-looking Tully peers out. Jimmy scans the street. Empty, except for a cloud of smoke and dust going down the street. Tully had seen a car coming slowly along the street and as it turned the corner the rear door opened and a long canister was rolled under the OP; luckily it bounced off the tin at the bottom and exploded harmlessly in the street. Tully had ducked when he saw what it was, which was just as well because the inside roof of the OP was dotted with little shrapnel holes.

The radio is going crazy. Everyone wants a piece of the action. Company HQ are demanding a detailed report before we even know the full account, and the O.C. is round with the C.S.M. poking around and generally getting in the way. We've already checked the OP structural supports for any sign of damage and found none, so there's no need for a lengthy post-mortem. Tully gets torn off a strip or two for not getting the number of the car, but if he had got it he would not be around to tell us what happened anyway. You can't have it all ways.

Life returns to the level of normality we have grown accustomed to with Paul explaining to Harvey, the six-foot white rabbit, that there was nothing to be afraid of and the O.C. looks a little worried. Tully's stutter has got a little worse, and so he's in for a whole pile more leg pulling.

It's patrol time again. From this location we are required to carry out clearance patrols of the immediate area and up to the other OP at Fort Cross.

Jimmy takes over the desk and we are out into the fresher air. Across the Crumlin and through into the Shankill. The comforting weight of the S.L.R. and the steady rhythm of swinging legs. The freedom of feeling the wind against your face after hours of being cooped up in the tense sewer of the OP. We make our way along the now familiar streets, on up towards the other Fort. On our way, checking a derelict here, a person there; note the cars in the area for any changes; note the comings and goings from the houses of personalities that we are keeping a watch on. All of this is done in the casual way of experience. The street becomes a living animal. We know where to hide. We can feel the varying tensions, the vibrations given off by guilt complexes, the cunning, the hate and the pity. It's a tangible thing. Some days your skin crawls and the whole patrol seems very vulnerable; on other days, like today, we stroll around casually, even exchange pleasantries with the locals.

Most of the houses on the peace line are all gutted. Only the old and the foolish live here. The sectarian violence of the late sixties has left a permanent physical scar across the city, with miles of corrugated tin separating communities who speak the same language, do the same jobs and live in the same square mile of city. We've given up moralising now and just get on with the job.

"Hello 33 Bravo, this is 33 Lima, open backdoor, over."

"33 Bravo, Wilco, out."

We approach the Fort via the back entrance, up through an alleyway between the derelicts. Constant and random patrols are vital to ensure that the area is kept clear at all times. The back door is open when we arrive, with one of the Toms standing away to one side with S.M.G. at the ready. As soon as he sees who it is he relaxes and we step into the tiny back yard. I check the position of the intruder alarm and we walk through to the house. Hookey's full of good cheer, enjoying the status of OP commander, and the easy chat flows around the fetid air of Fort Cross. It is the favourite of the two, primarily because of the tea and cakes that are brought in by two old ladies every night at around eleven. However, with all the friendliness there is still the underlying feeling of distrust and everyone is always on their guard in case some information is let out. This can work to our advantage and if there is anything we think the opposition should know, we let it slip in the conversation.

A short break and we're out through the front entrance for a tour around the graveyard of the Holy Cross church. During an exchange of gunfire one day in the handover week, the priest was seen to be putting pieces of material on the iron railings of the church grounds. We later figured the meaning of the different colours and found a simple code was being used to keep the Ardoyne population informed as to the position of troops on the ground. During that week, two Light Infantry soldiers had been killed and one seriously wounded, all within twenty metres of the church.

We stalk through the graveyard, one moving, the other down and watching. Working in pairs. The buddy system. Headstones stand mocking in silent testimony to our fears. Anywhere else and this would be a place of peace and magic, of beauty and wonder. The tall proud pillars of stone are a landmark, visible from all over the city. To us, another hazard to be negotiated with care. Lying on the damp ground listening to the roar of traffic, the bustle of a big city, watching Pte. Larkin get up and carefully thread his way through the bushes and shrubs nosing the barrel of his S.L.R. before him, head turning from side to side. It all seems so improbable. Knowing there are ten rounds of 7.62 ammunition in my magazine and that the rifle is cocked, brings me back to the reality of the situation.

These clearance patrols are short and we are soon back in the OP. Later, Hookey will take a patrol out to clear his back area, and still later, one from the base will look in. The Forts are vulnerable and must be watched at all times. In the other Company areas they also have their own positions. In the Old Park district, it is above the old chip shop and so it is called just that. The chip-shop OP. In the New Ardoyne, there is a junction of roads and this is known as the Rings OP. Out of all of them, it is the Rings that so far has had the most action with regular short-lived firefights with snipers. In one such incident, a young boy was caught in the crossfire and died of his wounds. The press and T.V. had a field day, with both the Army and the I.R.A. denying that he was killed by one of their rounds. We came out of it best by virtue of the fact that the boy's uncle, who had been driving the car at the time, had changed his story between the two news programmes on the T.V. that night. It was easy to claim that he had been subjected to intimidation during the time between the two bulletins. Nobody gave a shit about the poor little bastard. Propaganda, that's what it's all about, and we play the game as viciously as everybody else. Human life becomes graded by the ability to be used for maximum publicity. Propaganda and publicity, the weapons of a twentieth-century society.

The most effective OPs are the covert ones and we're getting pretty good at them. The most difficult to carry out successfully and potentially extremely dangerous, they are, without doubt, also great fun if you discount the discomfort and squalor that have to be put up with, in order to gain maximum effect.

Covert OPs are set up in either occupied or derelict houses overlooking areas of particular importance or just acting on information received. One was carried out by Support Company the other week which resulted in three kills and two seriously wounded gunmen. They had collected on a street corner and started handing out weapons prior to an attack on an Army patrol. The OP was twenty metres away across the road, and after the initial challenge, opened fire. One man escaped the hail of bullets, the others were not so lucky. Paras 5, I.R.A. 0.

The coverts in our area were centred on the drinking clubs and good old U.D.A. headquarters. Days spent peeing into plastic bags, shitting into same. Eating cold out of tins. Never talking except to pass messages on the radio at the dead of night. Videotape whirring quietly, to be watched later. The personalities logged, crosschecked and filed for later use.

We have a Company within the Battalion, D. Company, that are supposed to be the specialists at this type of thing. One patrol is attached to each rifle Company and are considered cowboys by the lads. On one occasion, the platoon commander on one covert called for assistance in the middle of the night. A Saracen was rushed round with the stand-by section all ready for some action, when they found out that the guy had been crawling round the landing of the derelict they were using, looking for a place to pee, when he fell through some rotten boards and broke his ankle. Needless to say, it took a long time for him to live that one down.

So far this tour we've done more damage to ourselves than the I.R.A. has. The strain of constant tension, restricted movement and exhaustion is beginning to show. Tempers become shorter, sporadic fights break out. Roll on R. and R.

The hours crawl past, dragging up to midnight when I will finally get to sleep. Crashed out on my bunk, not even bothering to take my boots off. Heavy eyelids droop over bloodshot eyes. Have another cigarette. Get up and walk around a bit. Pick up a radio and take a trip up to the OPs again.

It's a dark night in Belfast. The quiet streets are framed by the slits of the OP. Surrealistic shadows stretching down pavements, marching past battered doorways, peeking into private misery. What's going on behind the curtained windows? Screwing in number 56? Making bombs in number 57? Planning a raid on a post office in number 58?

On a couple of streets children still play in the dirt of the gutter. Pushed out by parents screwing in the only bedroom. The lonely cry of a baby. The raised voices of a couple arguing. The drunken singing of a depressed community.

Fuck them all, I'm going to bed!

0700 hrs. June 1973

In the talk
Between
Us
There is no
Communication.

They've been bullshitting us again with crap about how we're winning the war. The new C.O. is running around like a chicken with his head cut off and I'm standing here on the street doing the interminable census.

"Get to know your local community." Bullshit.

Hearts and minds, comes the never-ending cry from the politicians. Get a fucking rifle in your hand and get out here, comes the never-ending reply from the Toms on the streets. The Battalion before us did the same thing, as the one before them, as the one before them etc., etc. Where does all this information go to? Or is it just stored to keep a tally on how great a work rate each Battalion achieves?

"Make friends with your local U.V.F. gunman." Well why not, at least then we'll know what the hell he's up to.

The Shankill. Big, sprawling, vicious. A high percentage of unemployment and crime. The whole area being under the unofficial protection of the U.D.A. and run by gangsters. A community just as suppressed by fear as the Catholics in the Ardoyne. The methods used to control them just the same as the I.R.A. use. Kneecappings, beatings and in some instances, torture and death.

Census patrols. The chance for tea and biscuits if you get to the right part of the area; and for some the chance of a quick screw with some randy Irish housewife kinky for a bit of Para dick complete with flak jacket and boots on. Me? I never touch 'em mate!

Random musings on a street corner, whilst waiting for Paul to finish chatting to the reticent woman in number 13. We take it in turns to chat at the doorstep, otherwise the constant repetition of questions can drive you just a little crazy.

"Excuse me, madam, would you mind answering a few questions? We are taking a census and want to check the names of everyone in the house."

"Youse always round, youse fucking Army bastards." Just another way of saying "Well, we have been done before, you know." It doesn't matter what you think about it, lady, you're going to answer the questions anyway.

In one house, a timid woman with a couple of snotty-nosed brats cries silently into a handkerchief. Her husband is serving time in Long Kesh for arms offences. You would feel pity if there wasn't a doubt about her tears and innocence. Under the cushions on the settee, filthy nappies linger still with the shit in them and the whole house reeks of stale piss. She's talking about nothing in particular, just on and on in an endless stream of self-pity. We sit and listen politely, waiting for a suitable opportunity to escape. Hearts and minds. Be nice, encourage the talk, something might slip out. The tea, served out of dirty, cracked mugs, tastes like dishwater and there have been instances of ground glass being mixed with the sugar. What a place this is.

I was really quite a nice guy before I came out here. Now the frustrations are building and the inner violence seethes below the surface waiting for an opportunity to escape. Looking at this pathetic woman, I'm not thinking about the broken home or the deprived background. I'm thinking, *I wonder what she's like between the sheets?* Swear at me, lady, and I'll crack you so hard your teeth will fall out.

What's happened to me? Belfast, that's what.

The city breathes its own cancer and we are right in the middle of it all. Build an outer casing around your emotions, enjoy the sense of power, revel in the excitement of the chase, the aggro, the gun battles. Enjoy it. Enjoy it.

Paul collects Harvey and we continue the route. Harvey is becoming a personality now and we all play the game, talking to him, covering him across the streets, a gap even opens in the middle of the patrol. Paul introduces him at every doorway. The locals are too bemused to say a thing. The Shankill Road, wide, bustling with life and energy, the heartland of the U.D.A. and U.V.F., Tartan gangs and other fringe groups. Lined with shops, bars, gutted buildings, concrete-filled barrels on the edge of the road to stop car bombs being parked outside pubs and clubs. Listless stares from the vacant faces of the unemployed, standing around waiting, always waiting.

Memories of standing here during the Orange Day marches, cut off from the other members of the patrol, feeling vulnerable and scared. Thousands lining the street cheering, drinking, singing, not worrying about me at that moment.

Now it's an ordinary day. A weak sun is throwing grey shadows across the tarmac, fleeting glimpses of pinched faces in passing cars, images of the High Street at home on any day, housewives shopping, babies in prams, teenagers in calf-length bell-bottomed jeans and boots, kicking cans along the pavement. Buses disgorging passengers, taxis full to overflowing, meandering with the daily traffic of businessmen, salesmen and what else? The grating sound of ghetto Irish slicing through the hubbub and digging deep into my mind.

The patrol weaving in and around the shoppers, part of the scene and yet separate. An essential part of the character of the place and yet an unwelcome intrusion. We forget that the first shots fired at the Army came from so-called "Loyalist" guns, and that the first Army casualties were inflicted by the people calling themselves part of England. It's all a question of whatever suits at the time.

We've been long enough on the main drag now and we slip through a maze of alleyways to another aspect of the locality. Still the same housing, but the essence of the character of the Shankill heightened by these clusters of streets. Good neighbourliness is not apparent here at all. Confidential whispers from spiteful women about the goings on at the end of the row.

"That Michael Hare is a real bad one. He's the man around here."

"The man" is usually a weedy little runt who makes a habit of beating his wife regularly. Not that that has much bearing on the matter, but he may well have sworn at the woman now confiding. Telephone calls have been made to the robot phone for no other reason than the caller wants to see the person turned over by a house search at two o'clock in the morning.

Knock on the door. Answered by a prematurely old woman. Go through the usual questions and get invited in.

"Cup of tea?"

"Yes please."

"Oh, it's nice to see the Paras back again. Give the boyos hell." Nod in agreement.

"Of course, you won't have any trouble here. Not in the Shankill. We all support the Army, you know."

"Well, that's nice to know." Lying.

"Oh yes, my father was in the Army during the war. Fought for England."

"Really?" Not believing a word. Not caring. We've heard it all before. 1 Para had one of its biggest contacts in Belfast right here in this street when two Landrovers were ambushed. They were lucky to get out of it.

"Of course, there are some bad people around, but they don't come from here."

Not true. I wonder if she really believes all that she is saying, or whether the 'boyos' have such a hold that anyone will say anything just for a quiet life. Well, you couldn't blame them. We know that this woman has a retarded son. In fact, the district has a special bus that picks up the mentally deficient in the area and takes them off to a special school.

Poor little buggers. Not knowing what it's all about. Smiling empty smiles. Confused minds trying to separate people and to understand right and wrong. The lads take the piss unmercifully with comments like:

"Hello madam, who's your monkey?"

Anything to spark a reaction. Anything to hurt, to scar for the crime of being a part of this community. Nobody is innocent in our eyes.

We must have our revenge.

Hearts and minds. It's difficult to do. Switch off the feeling, and smile, keep smiling. Smile at the abuse. Smile at the hate. Smile. Smile. Smile.

"You boys here for much longer? Had your R and R?"

Here it comes, the gentle probing for information and yet there is no need, as they probably know more than we do anyway. There is no such thing as a secure telephone in Belfast, so the questions are only a preliminary to the revelation that a particular Battalion is going to take over when we leave and on a particular day. At first it was unnerving but now we just smile and say, *"Really, they don't tell us anything you know."* Not that they're fooled for an instant, but it's all part of the game.

"Where do you come from son, I've got a sister lives in Liverpool."

Now that really is a surprise. The only city in England that has the majority of ferry traffic. Day trip and stayed forever. Nod in assent and make noises of encouragement. Have another biscuit, slurp down the tea, check my watch, nod to Paul and leave.

Another house, another face and a different reaction. The same look, the same sound, a different approach. Images of living on the bread line. Threadbare carpets, tattered clothes, whining children, cans of beans and piles of washing left for weeks. Rusting scrap in the small back yards, overflowing toilets, grimy curtains on opaque windows. Their lives lurching from incident to incident, feeding on the scraps of hope scattered by politicians eager for power. The men in suits and ties, making a living from the misery of others. Using them to feature in the news. We are all victims. Every last one of us in the city of destruction.

The Toms are yawning on the pavements and in the bushes. Hours of census taking, sapping the interest and destroying the concentration. Time for a change. Call for a Saracen on the radio. Drive to a different part and out patrolling again.

The temptation is to cut short the patrol, or to move nearer to base so that you're in, the moment your time is up. It becomes a monotony of clock-watching. If I had wanted to knock on doors for a living, I would have been a salesman.

Lunch at Leopold Street for the first time in weeks. A brief respite before putting in a court appearance in the afternoon. Earlier in the tour, one of my men had been hit by a drunken driver whilst on a routine V.C.P. on the Old Park Road and Crumlin Road junction. It was late on a wet night when the car came hurtling down the road, scattering soldiers and burying itself in the side of the Saracen. One of the Toms was hit by the car, carried twenty metres down the road and thrown onto the Saracen, tossed over it and landed a further thirty metres down the road. At first we thought he must be dead, and the driver of the vehicle too, but him we didn't care about. As it was, the driver of the car was just dazed. He was quickly removed from the car, bundled into the back of the Saracen and taken care of. Women were screaming in the street, Toms were threatening to shoot everything in sight. Turmoil in a few short moments.

The outcome was the end of the Army career of the soldier, who survived but had a badly broken leg and multiple injuries. The court case was to send the driver away for dangerous driving, drunken driving and the rest. The case was going to be interesting because there had been counter-allegations by the car driver of brutality and assault. Whether he suffered his broken jaw and nose plus other minor injuries in the crash or afterwards seemed to be a matter of conjecture. The truth is buried in the haze of forgetfulness that surrounds most incidents in the city.

The Crumlin Road courthouse is opposite the main prison and on the edge of our area. Many soldiers know the inside only too well. We must be the only Army in the world that has to account for every minute of time, every action taken. Guilty until proved innocent, my Lord. Yellow cards with instructions on when to open fire. White cards on arrest procedures. Another white card on the use of P.V.C., baton rounds, and yet another on how M.79 grenade launchers can be used.

Will you please stop the battle, I have to consult my yellow and white cards.

The O.C. has dropped off again at the table, going unnoticed amongst the small talk.

"Confidential reports due in at the end of the week, young sirs." Brian, the C.S.M., keeping the admin ticking over.

"Don't ask the Officers, they haven't done the joined-up writing course, yet." The Colour Sergeant.

Meaningless mouthings. In-jokes. Leg-pulling. Cursing, swearing but with very little to say. Brian put the whole thing into perspective: "I don't want to know you, because to me you will be just another number when I shovel what's left into a body bag."

His way of saying "I don't want to get involved because I don't want to get hurt." He's tried to tell me to do the same, but when you work with men constantly, day in day out, the personal involvement is bound to be there, however much you disguise it.

My platoon's good because we are all involved. All this and chips too.

The court is a joke. The case a farce. We have to drop the serious charges or be faced with a long, drawn-out trial with assault and brutality running riot. The guy gets off and we're back to the streets.

A change this time though. A trip round the U.D.A. clubs, to chat up the locals in their own environment. Forced conversation, with no point of contact. Shifty eyes, furtive looks, noses buried in mugs of beer.

"Hello Lieutenant, come in. Will you have a drink?"

"Mr. McKracken. How are you? I see the bar's doing well, any problems during the week?"

"Oh Lieutenant, you know that there is never any trouble in the Shankill. Why, some of your lads come from round here."

"That's true." And I wouldn't trust any one of them, either.

"Are you comfortable up at Leopold Street?" Knowing we are not.

"Oh yes, we have really got the place fantastic." Knowing he knows that is nonsense.

"You have got the bar done out nicely." Thinking that for a fleapit it is not bad.

"We try, you know." He knows I'm taking the piss.

The verbal sparring continues. Outwardly a show of interest and friendliness. Inwardly knowing that given half a chance we would happily turn this place over. There's usually one spokesman in the group, answering questions for all the men, who are suddenly taking a very deep interest in the newspapers, or finding that the beer has reached their bladders far quicker than anticipated.

Our eyes are not on the man we are talking to, but roaming around the room. No need to try and be furtive about it any more. The illusions of co-operation vanished some months ago, now we try and gain as much information as possible. There is not much to be gained, of course, the interesting characters having been warned of an Army patrol in the neighbourhood, and secreted themselves in some back room or moved out by car. We know this and it doesn't matter because there is always someone who wants to shop another, sometimes for reasons of personal gain, sometimes out of pure spite. We are the poor suckers on the ground who get the feeling that some of the nasties are kept in power by the authorities from expediency. Better the devil you know, etc. This makes life on the street all the more difficult.

Eventually you lose track of all the secret squirrels lurking around, trying to pass themselves off as part of the community. Cowboys in civilian clothes, as if the local community don't know that someone has been inserted in their midst. They are purely diversionary, but I wonder if they know that? With the number of Irish in the Army who actually live in these areas, it is just not possible to use regular troops in infiltration roles without the locals knowing about it. Christ, it's so easy to spot a squaddie even with long hair and dirty jeans.

It doesn't take long to tire of the banter and we come to the real reason for the visit to the club. Some of the local lads have recently taken it upon themselves to spark a few incidents of bottle throwing, crashing V.C.P.s and other sundry silliness, so before it gets out of hand we try and enlist the aid of the U.D.A.

"Sammy, there have been a few nasties in this area over the past week or two. Do you know anything about it?"

"Really Lieutenant? Well, I didn't know that now. I'll just have to take your word for it."

"Well, perhaps the word might go out that we don't appreciate the invitation to have a free-for-all. You know what that leads to?"

"Well now Lieutenant, I really don't know what I can do about it. I'll see if I can talk to some of the parents."

"Thank you, Sammy, we appreciate it."

The word will go out swiftly, the offenders found and either the proverbial kneecap job or just a plain beating. The clubs don't particularly want to be raided at this moment as business is going well, especially on the supplies of stolen booze. Profits are high and the living for the local "god-fathers" is good. Policing by proxy.

When it suits us we'll raid the clubs; they know this, but the longer they can be kept open the better the nest egg at the end of the day.

The clubs. Some legal with licences to serve alcoholic drinks, a majority illegal. The illegal ones run by the U.V.F. and its fringe groups.

The clubs. Where plots are hatched to drive the Catholics out of Northern Ireland. In the Ardoyne they exist to bolster the cause of the I.R.A.

The clubs. Breeding grounds for discontent, anarchy and bloodshed.

The clubs, the clubs, always the clubs.

Private thoughts compartmentalised. Private emotions suppressed. Hearts and minds. Don't forget what you're doing.

"No really, it's a six-foot white rabbit." Paul, straight-faced with a captive audience, who are now looking visibly scared.

"What do you mean, you fuckin' can't see him?" At first they laugh.

"What the fuck are you laughing at? I don't see anything funny."

The smiles die away and an unease spreads through the place. Well, would you laugh at a potential nut with a rifle? The lads are enjoying the joke hugely. Light relief in the interminable round of forced smiles and charm.

Charm! How do you charm a spitting cobra?

Back at Leopold Street, complaints are beginning to drift through about intimidation to women in the area.

"He swore at me and made fun of my Michael."

"They came into my house and tried to rape me."

What time, what day, what did he look like. Tense in case they can link in a time that my patrol was in the area. Most times they get it wrong, their sense of timing no good. The local priest is the one that usually comes with the tales. Show him a copy of the log and send him away satisfied.

Talking to the priest is the most disliked chore in the base. He's old, bigoted and rambles for hours about how good the people are.

"Wonderful people, the Irish. Warm, generous to a fault." Duck as another salvo of bricks, bottles and petrol bombs come hurtling over the roof-tops.

"Kind, considerate, family-loving people."

Watch the middle-aged housewife impassively. "Youse fucking bastards. I hope your children all die. I hope some big nigger's fucking your wife, God rot your soul."

"Oh yes, Father, we know and have enjoyed the hospitality of the people." Does he really believe this crap? He's still talking.

"I know some of the lads like to have a bit of fun every now and again, but that is understandable." I wonder if I'm hearing right or that something has tripped my brain and jumbled all the words around.

"Now with the Catholics, it's different of course. They are born with a violent nature. They must be stopped and the only way is for you to go in and shoot the ringleaders. We know who they are and if you don't do it then there are people here who will. Never you fear." Wow, some man of God this.

"What we need are the B. Specials back again."

This really is beginning to get to me and if it wasn't for the fact that I had been ordered to talk to the guy and "be nice, Clarke, be nice," then he would have been out on his ear a long time ago. That's Belfast. Everything arse about face. Nothing normal any more. Ignore it or go gently loopy.

An N.C.O. in Flax Street Mill went into the vehicle park and blew his brains out with a pistol. One of my soldiers was posted to a desk job when he was found to be talking to himself in an OP. He had cocked his rifle and was waiting to shoot anyone that happened to be walking down the street. Eighteen and cracking. We have a catch phrase going round the Company: "You can't crack me, I'm a rubber duck." Everyone walking around quacking at each other.

Quack, quack. It's even found its way onto the Battalion radio net, to be accompanied by that famous character, the "phantom whistler". The Battalion Ops officer is going spare. The ducks and the phantom whistler even answer routine radio checks. All measures to stamp out the breach in radio discipline fail. The ducks and phantom whistler live on to provide amusement to the lads and fuel the anger of the idiots on the Ops Desk. Hearts and minds. Ours this time. Quack, quack.

Clive is selling me battleships at three in the morning. I'm deciding on the colour and optional extras. Both of us fantasising on an air strike straight down the Shankill Road, complete with mortars and a tank for good measure. After all, we don't want any survivors, do we?

As time drags on, the whole camp is praying for a contact. For an opportunity to shoot at anything on the street, pump lead into any living thing and watch the blood flow. Toms sitting in their overcrowded rooms putting more powder into baton rounds to give them more poke; some insert pins and broken razor blades into the rubber rounds. Buckshee rounds have had the heads filed down for a dum-dum effect, naughty, naughty, but who's to know when there are so many spare rounds of ammunition floating about. Lead-filled truncheons, magnum revolvers, one bloke has even got a Bowie knife.

Most of the N.C.O.s and officers are aware that these things are around and if they aren't, then they shouldn't be doing the job. We have spent months and years training, learning from pamphlets called "Shoot to Kill", "Fighting in Built-up Areas" and others. So now, we're let loose on the streets trained to the eyeballs, waiting for a suitable opportunity to let everything rip.

A few kills would be nice at this stage, good for morale, good to inject some new life into the jaded senses of the Company. Listen to me, rambling on about how a few deaths will solve the man-management problems. I know I'm thinking these things but no longer seem to care. Let's do it. Let's stir it a bit.

Thinking back to the ten o'clock news and the piece of film about a car bomb in the city. One of the Toms was on an S.P.G. patrol when the warning came through, and was busy clearing the area when the thing went off. The film shows him walking casually down the street when it blows and he is engulfed by a cloud of smoke and dust, to emerge a few seconds later still walking casually along.

"Just look at that," he cries. "Holy fuck just look at that." The rest of the Toms are sitting around the box shaking their heads.

"Wow, oh wow, wow, wow."

"Shit. Crazy cunt." Wonder in their eyes. Wish I'd been there.

Strange city. Get into a gunfight, kill a few people, then relax and watch the replay on the box. At the moment, it's still the interminable census. Street-walking, door-knocking, brain-draining boredom.

Hearts and minds.

2200 hrs. July 1973

Warm night,
Cool head,
Sore feet.
The shot you don't hear
Is meant for you.

Support Company have been enjoying themselves over the past few weeks with a couple of contacts and a good publicity-earning kill in the Old Ardoyne. A gunman complete with Armalite rifle just about to zap at a foot patrol. He never got the butt into the shoulder. There was also a contact that we came superficially into when a stolen car was chased down the Crumlin and into the Shankill. It was eventually stopped, the occupants were turned onto the street and a seriously wounded terrorist was found lying on the back seat. By the time the patrol commander had finished a lengthy P. Check, the guy on the back seat was going cold. What a pity. Never mind. We all cheered and laughed, of course. One more of the bastards down.

Apart from the odd low-velocity round and occasional scuffle, there has been little going on in our area. Although to date we have had the largest number of finds of arms and ammunition, it has caused little upset amongst the people. We've never been too friendly anyway, so any cooling off of attitude really doesn't bother us. In fact, there are those among us who would dearly love to stir the pot a bit and crack the self-satisfied smugness of the U.D.A.

Hookey and I have decided upon a little plan of action.

"O.K., Hookey, on every late-night patrol, after midnight every swinging dick that moves in the area gets the complete treatment. Hands against the wall, complete body search. The lot. Any cunt that gets a bit mouthy, on the deck, spread-eagled. We don't particularly want to lift a whole pile because TAC will only let them go."

"O.K., boss." Bright gleam in his eyes.

The choice of after midnight is logical, in that anyone moving around that late at night in a hard area, was probably on the fringes of the outlawed organisations; otherwise they would not have the nerve to be out and about.

Funny things happen in the dead of night in the Shankill.

Standing around in the Ops Room looking through the personalities file, when a call comes through on the radio. A panic voice, indistinct amid the crackle of static. Immediately the whole atmosphere changes. The stand-by section commander, half-asleep in his chair, suddenly wide-awake and half-way out the door to get the section ready and Saracen fired up. Within two minutes they are sitting in the Saracen and I've joined them, with the information that a patrol has been ambushed in the Shankill Road. No other information bar the exact location.

"Straight down to the Shankill, turn left and up to the Agnes Street junction. Go like hell." I'm shouting into the driver's ear above the roar of the engine.

"When we get there, I'm dropping three of you off short of the turn and want you down in fire positions covering the rear. Jimmy, take the other three round the immediate area. There's a back-up on its way as soon as they get a Pig out to pick them up." Shouted orders. Thumping heart. Eyes wide in expectation. Cocked weapons. Holy fuck, this is it!

There's a grey Morris 1800 in the middle of the street. Confusion. A Military Policeman kneeling beside the front wing. Another appearing from a doorway.

"What the fuck are you doing here?"

"We were just doing a routine car patrol, checking on stolen vehicles."

"You were what?" I'm incredulous. I don't believe my ears. Two M.P.s casually driving down the Shankill in the middle of the night in a civilian car in full uniform.

"Oh, forget it. What happened?"

"As we were driving along, we were fired at from down there." Pointing away to the south of the road. "We stopped and returned the fire."

"Did you hit anything?"

"No."

"How many rounds?"

"They fired about four or five, I think. My mate loosed off his magazine."

"What, the whole lot?"

"Yes."

Thirty-odd rounds sprayed into the darkness. What would they have done if the gunmen had stayed around for a second go? Crap-hats.

Jimmy's returned from his snoop around and found nothing. Not even a sign of life in the vicinity. Anti-climax. Another fucking anti-climax. The tension screw winds a little tighter.

The lads are giving the monkeys hell. The back-up patrol has arrived along with the O.C., the C.O., the Battalion Ops officer and God knows what else. If only they would all stay out of the way and let us get on with it. The new C.O. in particular, is being a pain in the arse. Career stamped all over himself like a cheap tattoo. A boring little man with a boring little mind.

How is it that we are controlled by a lot of fucking idiots? For some reason the best officers never reach the top positions. It certainly gets to the men and the image of the chinless wonder drinking gin and tonic in the Mess, is further enhanced by guys like this one. We've got a good Battalion with great soldiers and some really good officers, and then there is this clown.

I manage to get my guys back into the Saracen and we are meandering slowly back to Leopold Street via the back streets in low gear at high revs. The high-pitched whine of the Saracen in low gear is shattering, and guaranteed to wake even the heaviest of sleepers. Wake up you bastards! If we don't sleep, you don't. A couple of guys walking down the street with a girl. Great!

Pile out of the Saracen, rifles levelled.

"Assume the position. Hands on the wall, fingers spread, now get those legs apart. Afraid you'll drop something?"

The girl is standing still, not saying a word. All our questions meeting no response. They're more afraid of what the "boys" will do to them than what we have to offer. Soon change that, sunbeam. The dull thud of an idly swung baton up between the legs. Gasp of pain.

"Who told you to move, cunt?" Baton swings again, cracking hard onto a kneecap. Shrug from the Tom in my direction. "Looked as if he was going to hit you, boss."

A body search with hands up hard between the legs. Squeezing testicles. Tears in the eyes. Fear in the eyes. Hopelessness in the face turning slowly to anger and hard resolve. That's good mate, get angry, try something. Better still, go tell your mates.

"What are you doing with these two specimens, love? Why not come back with us? Bet they don't know what it's for. Nice girl like you."

Hungry-eyed Toms, with open crudeness, visually undressing the girl.

"Is she a good fuck, mate? Do a good blowjob, does she?" Chuckles and laughter.

"O.K. lads, you've had your fun, back in the vehicle. Let's go." Back to Leopold Street. Back to the cocoon. Back to the freaky non-talk of people grouped together for too long, to a private world behind a blanket stretched over the opening of a bunk, to the constant banter and false bravado.

The "street" is the reality and the unreality. The centre of the universe, the beginning and the end of time. The whole spectrum of all human existence in full living colour written on the walls, scored with the thump of explosive, photographed in the mind of a diseased body. Replayed every day, relived with boredom. We live in the commercial break of a battered building. Selling our morality to ourselves over and over again, with the help of war books, films, T.V. and sleep. Don't think of the rights and wrongs, just let the beast rise and enjoy the primeval passion.

An Army sniper who had just shot and killed a terrorist on the street was asked by a woman reporter what it was like to shoot someone.

"You just squeeze this little thing here," he said. She went away with the wrong impression, but no doubt just what she wanted to hear. The soldier sadly shaking his head. We are here to create the news for a hundred poised pens and ready cameras. To provide a nation with its quota of violence, to give people the chance to shake their heads, others to organise marches, pressure groups and all the other paraphernalia of a well-organised growing industry. Northern Ireland is an industry, providing reporters with the opportunities to further their already stagnant careers, for social workers to martyr themselves on the unsympathetic conscience of an unimaginative nation. An entertainment without interlude. To hell with the lot of you.

The O.C. has us into the briefing room again. A club raid is on tonight. Great, comes the cry.

"Tony, your platoon with the Int. Section and C.S.M. We are not going to inform the R.U.C. until you are on the way. By the time they inform the club, you will be in there."

Major, we love you!

It has been suspected that on a number of occasions, when the R.U.C. have been informed prior to a raid, a tip-off has found its way to the target concerned. So now we have stopped letting them know until we are actually going through the front door. This method has led to the success of finding enormous amounts of arms and ammunition and other goodies. We don't trust any bugger, sometimes not even ourselves.

Club raid. Fantastic. Fantastic. This is going to be fun.

There is a woman living in a house just across the street from the location and it is obvious that as soon as a pile of Landrovers and Pigs and Saracens move off into the night that something is afoot and the word will spread like wildfire through the area. So we take it casually, and move out with two Landrovers as the main attack force first, the Pigs with the troops for the cordon to follow a little later. We are then going to join up and hit the club at the same time.

It's difficult to keep the excitement to a quiet level. All the Toms wanting to be part of the action and in the raid group. No such luck lads, the first people through the door will be the C.S.M. and Hookey, being the biggest. Or at least that was the plan. Everything is going smoothly, gliding gently down the street to meet up with the Pigs. As soon as the vehicles enter the street that the club is in, the U.V.F. sentries will have warned the occupants of a patrol in the area. We've got to be real fast.

We turn into the street. Foot flat down on the accelerator and hurtle towards the club. Watch as the sentries dive into the door. All chaos and noise now. The Pig slewing across the road disgorging soldiers who take up their positions, sealing off the junction and stopping all pedestrians.

Hookey and the C.S.M. pile out of the front seat, me right behind thinking now that I would much rather be a spectator. Too late.

Hookey hits the door with a flying kick and bounces back into the street. Fury doubled, he and Brian attack it with crowbars and finally break in where the noise of screams from the women and yelling abuse from the men, mixed with flying bottles, glasses, chair legs and whatever else is available, hits you like a wall. Some guy tries to crown me with a broken whisky bottle. I try to get my baton into a swinging position and eventually have to club him with my S.L.R.

Hookey's biting a bloke's nose virtually in half, and Brian's swinging lustily with his baton, yelling all the while. Two of my men manage to get to the rear of the club and the physical resistance begins to falter under the viciousness of the onslaught. More soldiers come in from the street, but there's still a little fighting going on. I cock my rifle and the place goes quiet.

"Right you bastards. Men on the floor, spread, women over on the right-hand side and for Christ's sake, shut up."

Some semblance of order now returning to the place. Bloody faces, spilled beer, broken bottles and glasses litter the floor. Sobbing women, shaking youths, cramped into this tiny den of hate and violence. The Pigs commandeered from other areas have arrived, and we start shuffling the human cargo up to Castlereagh for interrogation. Brian is standing over a guy seated in a chair in the middle of the room. He is very casually splashing whisky over a large split in the guy's skull, and then with great care and deliberation, starts to stitch him up.

"Where did you learn that, Brian?"

"On my D. Company medic's course. We spent a day on wounds and stitching." Doctor for a day. Expert in an instant. That's Belfast.

The tension has lifted somewhat and eases a bit more when one of the drunks, hitherto unnoticed, struggles to his feet and starts singing, slurring all the words together. A couple of the Toms pick it up and before long there is quite a little singsong. A brief connection through the gulf. Pigs are trundling off down the road one after another with pasty, blurry faces staring unfocused out of the back doors. Some still giving vent to their discomfort, hands tied together with the plastic tourniquets with non-slip grips. Very efficient and easier to carry around than handcuffs.

Outside, the cordon is working well except for one bugger screaming about maltreatment, only to get another wallop over the head with a baton and collapse insensible on the pavement.

"What's going on out here, for fuck's sake?" I ask.

"Just some cunt trying to get through the cordon saying that he is the local U.D.A. man around here and that he wants to see someone in authority. I tell him he's going nowhere and he starts to get naughty. So I belted him."

Fair enough, thinks I, and have a look at this guy. He's only one of the most influential blokes in the area, isn't he? Well, this will certainly keep the pot boiling for a little longer. There is certainly enough yelling and screaming going on out here, with cries of, *"Why don't you do this in the Ardoyne instead of picking on poor innocent people?"*

"We like to share it around. Don't want you all to feel you're missing something," replies a Tom.

Images of a political rally. Switch off the sounds and watch the mouths work, the fists shake, the eyes piercing like the sniper's bullet, knowing that all these people would, at this moment, gladly see you die. Not in the unreality of a news bulletin, but in the flesh, now.

Sullen-faced youths on the periphery, watching, gauging the feelings, counting down the time to positive action. The old game of "he knows that I know that he knows that I know." Chess with the lives of young teenage soldiers, fodder to sop the appetite of a thousand frustrated souls.

It's taken two hours to lift all the males from the club up to Castlereagh and we are just tidying up, searching the premises and generally making a nuisance of ourselves. Well, one thing is for sure, it's going to take them a long time to get this back together. Their bar stock liberally spread all over the floor, wiped off the shelves by a "careless" baton or rifle. Doors hanging off their hinges, tables and chairs broken, mirrors smashed and the Toms enjoying every moment of it.

Outside, the crowd gradually drifting away, muttering like a giant animal. The R.U.C. constables, who arrived late, are away in the background, not wanting any part of the proceedings. Most of them are Prots anyway, so don't want the local community to have any reason to be upset with them. None of the lads in our Company will have much to do with them, knowing the extent of their pay and overtime, plus the suspicion of graft from the Prot areas to turn a blind eye on certain occasions and to keep them informed as to what the Army are going to hit next. There is also the feeling that we are here running their war, getting killed to protect them from it. Going into areas that they just do not penetrate. Memories of taking an R.U.C. constable into the Ardoyne for the first time in four years. Memories of the look on his face, the smell of fear, the suspicion of damp at the crutch. All this and an eight-man patrol just to guard him. It's your war, get on with it.

The search finished, the team get into their Pig and drive slowly away up the road towards the Crumlin. The rest of us start to pack up, taking care because it is at this stage that you become most vulnerable to attack. Everything going smoothly. Just a minor disturbance with some kids flinging bottles, quickly taken care of and a semblance of peace returns to the area, floating on an undercurrent of increasing tension and hate.

Back in Leopold Street and everyone is taking the piss out of Hookey trying to break the door down. For us, it has worked off some of the feeling of impotence, drained, to some extent, the level of anger and violence that had been building up over the previous few months. There's nothing like a good fight to ease the savage in us all. But the light-headed euphoria of the moment is short-lived and the exhaustion of the past months catches up, creeping up the back of your neck to sock you between the eyes. It's flake-out in the Ops Room chair again, until the O.C. tips me out telling me that there's work to be done and no room for skivers. Get back on the street because there may be trouble after the raid.

Cheers, thanks very much.

Back out into the night, the armoured car moving slowly with the section on foot. Between the rows of vehicles lining the street, lit occasionally by the pale yellow glow of a streetlight, the rumbling sound echoing off the graffiti-covered walls.

FUCK THE POPE, screams one. U.D.A. RULE SHANKILL, another informs us, PARAS OUT, says one more, mirroring one in the Ardoyne.

Shadows hurry into alleys to vanish amid the wreckage of derelict houses, pounding hearts, hoping they have escaped notice.

Midnight on the Shankill, with occasional cars taking avoiding action at the sight of a patrol; those not quick enough are collared for a car search, to bear the brunt of accusing stares, sarcastic comments, in silence.

We caught them this time, before they managed to have any defence ready, so the area is quiet with no reaction.

Midnight on the Shankill, with the darkness lending a false sense of security to the patrol moving from street corner to street corner, tired eyes searching the blackness, tired minds beginning to switch off after twenty-four hours straight without sleep. If the opposition knew just how switched off we were at this moment, they would be round in an instant throwing everything they have. However, we have something far more valuable than a flak jacket or rifle. Our reputation. The myth that surrounds the "Paras", the image of supermen in smocks and denims. A load of rubbish, of course, we are just as vulnerable as everyone else, it's just that we don't seem to have the hang-ups about using force of the most vicious kind, whenever possible. You can't train people to the ultimate in death dealing and expect them to sit and do nothing. Memories of Bloody Sunday and the cheers that followed and the myths and awe that grew up around some of the Toms who claimed to have shot four or five apiece, and the eager ears listening to tales of the gunmen falling, of piling bodies into the back of Pigs, some still warm, but not for much longer. Remembering the anger and horror as we pulled bodies out of the remains of the Parachute Brigade Officers Mess after the bomb went off. A leg here, a hand there, part of a head, blood-covered clothes up in the trees.

Midnight on the Shankill, mind on the fact that I've missed a telephone call home, and perhaps I'll do it when I get back. Get my wife out of bed just to have someone to talk to. To feel again, before suppressing all emotion once more.

Mother, if you could only see me now!

Mind snapped back to the present with the distant thump and vibration of another car bomb in the city centre. They really have had a pasting so far this year. The centre of the city being slowly reduced to rubble, by the people who have to live in the place. Go ahead, destroy it all, then there won't be anything left for us to have to patrol around, to watch, to live in fear of. Go ahead, and if you need any help give us a shout, we'll help you bury the place.

Midnight on the Shankill, with Toms kneeling and lying in corners, crouched into doorways, S.L.R.s pulled into the shoulder, barrels pointing in the direction of sight, minds going through the number of possible sniper positions; the number of possible positions for a booby trap. If you really did as the book says and think of every permutation you'd soon go stark, staring mad with the fear of the number of possibilities there are. Be selective and stay sane. Trust in the second sense you have acquired since you've been here. Trust in your built-in survival kit, the gut feeling. Trust your men and hope that they trust you. Trust in whatever else is there, and hope that the remainder of the tour goes past quickly. But above all trust in yourself and your ability to do the job. If you don't, put on a front and make sure it's convincing.

Midnight on the Shankill and you are the only people in the world, and to everyone else you cease to exist, become part of the obscene graffiti, a mobile sculpture in the museum of what is Belfast.

For days now, my platoon has been hounding the locals without mercy, making sure that in every second of every day they are well aware of our presence.

We circle the clubs constantly, frisking the sentries until they eventually grow tired and retire inside. Stand for long moments staring up at the U.D.A. H.Q., which we are not allowed to touch but would dearly love to. At night, we're getting really good at digging out all the flotsam and jetsam and assembling them on the street in long rows with hands against the wall, legs spread, waiting for long minutes whilst I carry out lengthy P. Checks and detailed questions, just waiting for someone to say something out of place to provide the excuse for a bit of physical intimidation.

"You Prots have had it far too easy. We're going to change that."

"Youse making a mistake, sir."

"Really. What mistake is that?"

"The boys is not going to take it lying down."

"Is that a threat?"

"No sir, just a friendly warning."

"Just try it, sunshine, just fucking try it."

The friendly communication of two total strangers. Tonight we really are having fun, with about fifty guys lining the walls of the Shankill Road, their kidneys taking a pounding from batons whenever the mistake of making a protest is made. I'm walking slowly along the line asking questions, any that don't reply are taken quickly round the corner and the muffled thud and grunts can be heard clearly by the others still with their fingers on the wall. The message soon gets through and all sorts of useless information comes spilling out of their mouths. Mostly of no value, but now and again a confirmation of a face or a name. At this stage though, we really are not interested in any Intelligence sources, we want some action. We want to know where all the heavies are, where the arms caches are, not the fact that Sean O'Faherty has been robbing post offices for the past month.

"I don't know of any arms in the Shankill, sir, honest."

"How come we've turned up the biggest haul in any area for years, right in this street then?"

"Oh, I wouldn't know anything about that sir."

"Sure you don't."

It goes on for an age, and the more people that come down the street, the more we have adorning the walls. After an hour and a half of questioning the ranks are thinning, and most people walking the streets have been warned off by those we have released, and are taking detours down back alleys and side streets. However, we have another patrol circling the area that's busy picking up those that escape our net.

The women are being subjected to verbal abuse, and the men to a little physical contact. It's beginning to get a little out-of-hand, so I call it off and move the patrol off to let feelings cool a little. We want them to have a go at us, not have loads of court cases for grievous bodily harm charges, and have to go through the routine of not guilty, my Lord, and hope that we get the right judge.

The rest of the area is quiet as we move slowly back to Leopold Street, the odd person stopped and searched, the odd youth given a going over. At night, we come into our own, having brought patrolling to a fine art. We feel safe, unchallengeable, masters of the shadows. Quiet, creeping around the maze of dwellings and somewhere out there a pair of eyes behind a gun sight waiting for the right opportunity to fire one round. See one soldier die and then escape.

But not tonight, Paddy.

Not tomorrow, Paddy.

Because we've trained carefully Paddy...

It's turning into a typical Brecon night exercise. The wind has got up and the rain has given way to snow. Driving snow that blasts into your face, numbing nose and ears, stinging cheekbones. The last volley dies away and there is just the sound of the wind howling over the exposed night firing range.

"Watch and shoot. Watch and shoot." I feel for the trip-wire cables and hope I've got the right one. There's a loud bang off to my right as the section commander fires a Very pistol. The cartridge hisses up into the night sky, illuminating the range for a brief moment. Three targets appear over on the extreme right flank and the gun crew engage. In a matter of seconds the light fizzles out and the darkness descends once again. Behind me, the O.C. gives me a nudge and I pull one of the cables. There is a popping noise in front and then a brilliant white light from the trip flare. All the targets are illuminated, glowing eerily in the snow-filled dark of the Welsh night. The noise from the entire section firing is ear splitting and continues until the light finally dies. Total darkness descends once more.

"Section commanders check weapons all cleared." There is a pause whilst we listen to the sound of rifles being cocked and checked. The occasional curse from one of the N.C.O.s at some idiot who got the drill wrong. Once cleared, they file off the range and back to the comparative comfort of the hut.

On exercises like these I always feel a spare part. The Recruit Wing staff take over completely and run the range, usually with a superior attitude that belies their ineptitude. At times like these I would cheerfully stick one on these guys and take the consequences. They just make me want to throw up. Thinking all this whilst the O.C. belittles the N.C.O.s and the platoon. He's standing there in the dark in the snow, rabbiting on like an author of modern military tactics and leadership.

"Have you quite finished?" I ask. I'm angry. Really angry. And I don't need a lecture on how to handle my platoon from this juvenile.

"I have to make a report for the Depot," he says, smugly.

"Piss on your report," says I, and walk off. I really can't take any more crap. As far as I'm concerned, the lads worked very well under the most difficult circumstances. John, my platoon Sgt. falls into step beside me.

"Don't worry about it, boss. I've heard it all before. Most of the time it's just a load of bullshit. There's hot tea inside."

"Thanks." There's not much else I can say.

Inside the hut, the recruits are very subdued and it's not all exhaustion.

"Well done lads. I thought you managed pretty well under the circumstances. However this is what it's all about. The enemy won't pick nice sunny days to attack on. They'll come in the pitch black and in the worst weather, so you'd better get used to it here and now." No chorus of groans, just a shuffling silence as they move around trying to keep warm. "When you pass out of the Depot most of you will be going straight to Northern Ireland. The weather makes no difference as to whether you patrol or not." Again silence. "If you don't learn here, you'll die." No reaction. Ah well, perhaps I'll do better in the morning.

Next morning and I'm sitting in the cookhouse, shovelling greasy bacon and eggs into my mouth, washing it down with a pint of hot, sweet strong tea, discussing platoon admin with my Sergeant. Deciding how to fit in a kit inspection in between patrols so as not to disturb the sleep of the guys that have only just come in. It's just not possible, in the cramped derelict conditions with eight men to a room designed for two, to sleep in - if you turn over, another guy falls out of bed. Still it has to be done to ensure that the rifles are in top condition at all times, after all we don't want a stoppage just at the wrong time, do we chaps?

"Lt. Clarke, O.C. wants you, sir."

"O.K., be right there."

The O.C. is in the briefing room and has even got Clive down from the OPs to this O Group. Interesting. Well, not really, he only wants to inform us that the Company will be moving into Flax Street Mill for the last few weeks of the tour. Leopold Street location is going to be pulled down, as being unsafe to live in. Well, well, the powers that be have finally decided that the soldiers should have at least equal comfort to the prisoners in Long Kesh. Even that is not right, because to do that the Mill would need to be rebuilt entirely. So, startling news over, we drift back to our greasy eggs and bacon and continue the discussion.

There is a buzz going round the Ops Room and another call for me. It seems that some youths are getting a bit uptight on the Shankill Road and have commandeered a few buses and are setting up their own roadblock and generally getting out of hand. So it's out with the Pigs and Saracens to get the whole platoon loaded after a briefing, and off to the war. Baton guns are to the fore, wooden batons tucked into smocks and belts, snatch team ready. As we drive down, the jeers and yelled abuse from the locals gets louder and as we swing onto the Shankill the crowd have congregated at the junction of roads on the worst area of the Shankill. It figures.

"O.K. driver, head straight into the crowd, don't stop until I say so. Hello 33B and 33C, this is 33 Lima, I'm going down the centre, I want you two on either side. We'll go straight into them and when you see me turn, do the same and out with the snatch squads. Over."

"33B Roger out."

"33C Roger out."

"Listen lads, when we get out, I want an isolated area in the middle of the crowd and we will work outwards from there. Stay in pairs and for Christ's sake, look out for your mucker, let's have nobody getting separated from the rest."

Shouted orders in the confusion of noise and smell of the Pig, tense muscles, a stomach doing strange things, breathing shallow and fast, must take a deep breath.

Bottles smash on the roof of the Pig, scattering glass all over the road. A roaring bang from the turret as one of the Toms with a baton gun looses off into the crowd, the stench of cordite filling the inside of the Pig. As soon as the Pigs arrive people dive into doorways and run up side streets. Only the hardened remain behind and there must be a good five hundred of them collecting in the road.

The Pig drives straight into the middle, an opening forms as if by magic, those not quick enough are bowled over and thrown onto the pavements. The crowd scatters out to the side of the road.

Fragmented even more by the other two Pigs.

"Now!"

The driver throws the Pig sideways, nearly tipping over, and within moments Toms are spilling out into the street, batons flailing and whooping with aggression. The noise is deafening, screams from the women, threatening yells from the men. Identify the ringleaders is the first task. Isolate the troublemakers and scatter the rest, then deal with the smaller groups. The initial charge has worked and we have a good position, having opened the road and pressed the people back against the walls, but they are growing braver again as more people flood in from neighbouring streets, alleyways and spill out of the clubs, bringing crates of empty bottles to hurl.

"Fucking Army bastards."

"Paras out, Paras out."

The same chants over and over again, a scream goes up as a snatch squad leaps into the crowd and drags a man out by his hair, batons beating at his knees and kidneys. They're doing a good job diving into the seething mass and pulling out the ringleaders, slowly forcing back the turmoil, preventing any upsurge, killing it before it has a chance.

"They've killed him, they've killed him!" comes a shout from the other side of the street and I turn around to see Hookey throwing some guy into the back of a Saracen, bloody head and no hair. Hookey standing with something in his hand. Women screaming even louder now, convinced that the man has been scalped. He is dragged back out of the Saracen, and shown to the people. He hasn't been scalped at all, but when he was grabbed by the hair it came off in Hookey's hand, it being a toupee. A loud laugh ripples through the crowd and eases the tense situation somewhat.

Another ten minutes and the situation in the centre of the street has melted down to manageable proportions. I look up the Shankill and see at the top what must be a whole Company of the Gloster Regt., sitting at the Agnes Street junction. What the fuck are they doing there, I ask myself?

"O.K. you four, come with me. Hookey, I'm just going to take a stroll up the street to clear it. You handle things from this end. Right lads, I want you spread right across the road, we are going to clear this fucking thing and get all these bastards out of it. Jones, you have the baton gun, if any cunt gets in the way, blast him. Let's go."

I don't quite know what I'm doing. Walking straight up the middle of the Shankill Road in broad daylight. It's a good three hundred yards up to where the Glosters are hiding behind their Pigs; there are a good seven or eight hundred people gathered around, maybe more, all looking for the opportunity to get a gunman in and zap us, and I'm taking four men slowly up the street with no cover in broad daylight. Jesus.

As we move along, we toss the bottles and crates to the side of the road, move the beer barrels over and yell at the people to get back in their houses, clubs, pubs or wherever they came from. Sometimes if you bluff your way, it works. This time it did, but no way am I ever going to do that again! We arrive up at the Glosters, and stand sneering at them. Crap-hats!

They are all dressed up in the gear. Macralon shields, tin hats with visors pulled down, barbed wire spread over the road, crouching down waiting to endure the hail of rocks and bottles, so that people watching the news at home can say "Look what our lads are having to put up with." If you want to deal with a situation like this, get in amongst them, mates. Beat a few heads together.

"Who is in charge of this fiasco?" I ask the nearest Tom, who looks up at me as if in total agreement.

"Over there." Pointing to a weedy-looking chinless wonder hiding behind a Macralon-covered Landrover.

"How about getting this lot out of here?" says I, trying to be as tough as possible, with the *"I don't give a fuck if you are the C.O."*

attitude. The guy doesn't say very much, just starts moving his men out. Right, now to get on with the business in hand.

Down at the centre of the riot, Hookey has everything more or less under control. The repeated charges by the snatch squads have split the crowd up, nobody wanting to get their head busted, cowed somewhat by the violence of the troops. Just what was intended. Short and sharp. Get in amongst them and sort it out quickly, remove the initiative from them and take over control. The immediate problem is solved and traffic is able to move again; however, the word must have gone out because everyone is skirting the area. Mobile crowds of youths have now started to roam around the back streets, appearing as if by magic to hurl missiles at static patrols. It seems that they have been imported from outside the area especially for the occasion.

"Hello 33B, this is 33 Lima, send my Pig up, over."

"33B Roger, on its way. How's it going up there, boss? Over."

"33 Lima no problem. I'm just going to take a scoot around the side streets and dig out the troublemakers, over."

"33B Roger. I'll stay here and send the other Pig to give you some assistance, over."

"33 Lima Roger out."

Good old Hookey, just the sort of Sergeant every young officer should have. Company HQ have been on the radio fairly constantly since the little fracas started and so in between sorting things out on the ground, I also have to give a running commentary. Any moment now I expect to see the little figure of the C.O. rushing around and hope that he keeps his big nose out of it.

I've had time to think about myself whilst waiting for the Pig to arrive and notice that my legs feel weak and wobbly and I seem to be out of breath all the while. The Toms I have around me are looking a little pasty-faced waiting for something to happen. Itchy feet on a street corner, wanting the security of a crowd or armoured vehicle. Trigger fingers moving restlessly up and down the guard, eyes checking the safety catch, ears open for the crack of a round or rattle of a Thompson.

"Hello 33 Lima, this is 3 from 9, keep the Shankill open for the traffic, use two subunits to this end, over."

"33 Lima Roger out."

Well, that just leaves one section and one Pig to patrol the area and break up the roaming bands of rioting youths. Great.

"Hello 33 Lima, this is 33B, I got that and will keep 33C with me, out."

Here comes the Pig, clamber in and make sure the baton guns are in the best positions and move out. There's a crowd of youths just ahead as we swing round the corner, they turn and run when they see us.

"Get this fucking Pig moving," I yell into the driver's ear.

"I'm trying, I'm trying!" he yells back.

We've got to get close enough to be able to grab a few. Close enough so that the baton rounds will have maximum effect. That means less than ten metres away, closer if possible. The youths disappear round a corner and we pursue them, the Pig lurching round groaning under the weight of men and armour plate. As we straighten up we see that there must be about a hundred and fifty grouping in the road. In the Pig, there are eight of us crammed in.

"Straight into them, driver. Get those baton guns ready. I want a salvo as we go through on both sides."

The Pig ploughs into the living heap and the deafening crash of baton guns fill the air, for all the world like the short burst of a machine-gun. Screech to a halt, pile out and leap into the fray, batons swinging. As I move forward I raise my rifle and cock it. The Irish that did not run at the initial charge grab their injured and bolt into houses, alleys, anything to get away from the possibility of getting shot.

"Back into the Pig, lads."

Down the next street following the retreating mob and whenever we get close enough, out and charge again. So this is what all the fitness training is about.

Baton rounds are getting a bit short, but we seem to have taken the steam out of the riot, if we can just keep them moving and not let them have a chance to regroup then we've got it licked.

We are getting high on the violence now, the exhilaration of the chase, the feeling of uplift every time an Irishman goes down. We don't bother to take any prisoners, just zap them with the dick gun and trample over the prostrate forms. Let their own pick them up.

It's great, for the first time in months the shackles of restraint have fallen away and we're doing just what we want. It seems that the locals were not expecting the power of our reaction to the riot and are having to rethink their strategy.

"Hello 33 Lima, this is 3, return to this location, over."

"33 Lima Roger out."

We've been on the street three hours now. Three hours of minor battles, moving around following the mob, breaking it up to watch it form again, all the time protecting the remainder of the platoon who are keeping the Shankill open for traffic.

"Hello 33B, this is 33 Lima, acknowledge last from 3 and 33C to take over mobile cover, over."

"33B, Roger out."

Well, back to the Company location. Leave Hookey to it and find out what is going on.

Turning into Leopold Street, I see a great deal of activity surrounding the other vehicles. Peter, 8 Platoon Commander, is busy mustering his platoon, presumably to help us tie up the area. I'm wrong, he's going out to take over, with a D Company mobile patrol to cover the area surrounding the place we have set up as a firm base on the Shankill. At least that will allow us a little time to recoup some energy, get some food inside us and restock with baton rounds before going out again. Some of my platoon have been on the streets for eight hours straight, with only a few hours off in the early morning before starting this, and so far it looks as if it is going on for a long time. So no sleep for another night lads.

"Tony!" A shout from Peter. "What's going on out there?"

"There's a mobile riot touring the area, with the main aim, it seems, to try and block the Shankill and stop all traffic from moving. We managed to break it up but they are circulating in large groups. The main job is to keep them fragmented and stop them getting together in a group too large to handle. They are also trying to trap a patrol, so just drive straight through and don't stop until you have them running. Oh, and another thing, don't finish it before we get out again."

With a laugh, Peter is on his way again.

In the Ops Room everybody is asking questions at once, the noise of the radio adding to the confusion, until the O.C. clears the place and some semblance of order returns. After giving my report, it's time to wander zombie-like into the cookhouse and have a brew. Toms are sitting around still high on the fighting.

"Did you see that cunt go down when I swung the Pig door on him?"

"What about that other shit that Jimmy hit with the rubber dick gun, I thought he'd never get up from that."

"They need real bullets. That'll sort the bastards out."

It goes on, young lads carried away with the "rush" and light-headedness of the violence and lack of sleep. Kept high on the feeling of release from the long days and months of tension.

"O.K. lads, just quieten down a minute, we are going to be out again pretty soon so just get something to eat, sort out your kit and check your rifles because you may just have to use them."

After a cup of tea, I wander along to the briefing room and flop into a chair, mind a virtual blank after the hours of non-stop concentration on what Paddy is going to do next. The O.C. comes in and quietly sits down.

"Did you hear any machine-gun fire whilst you were out?"

"No. Why?"

"Well, we just had a call from the Glosters who reported to have heard what sounded like machine-gun fire from the Shankill."

I think a bit, trying to sort out what the O.C. is saying. It suddenly clicks and I laugh.

"That was no machine-gun, we were firing salvoes of baton rounds into the crowds."

"Well for God's sake tell us next time, you had TAC panicking like schoolgirls. It was as much as I could do to keep them away from the place."

"O.K. Major. Promise."

The door opens and Hookey's face appears.

"Hello, boss. We've just got back in. I've told the lads to get something to eat and get sorted out. Do we know when we're out again?"

I look at the O.C.

"In an hour. We'll see how Peter manages and if things start to get a little warmer, you'll be out sooner."

The O.C. leaves and a smiling Hookey sits down.

"Well boss, the blokes sure did well didn't they? No problem at all, even Tully got carried away and was really letting them have it. We've got a good platoon."

And we both sit grinning at each other like fools.

We are out sooner than expected, with the riots getting worse as the afternoon draws into evening, the shadows lengthening over the beer barrels, broken bottles, concrete-filled oil drums and whatever else they have managed to lay their hands on. A group of die-hards have got a barrier set up across the Shankill, and have set light to it, the orange glow silhouetting the dancing mass of people, busy tearing everything apart.

The C.O. is on the street now and we have been ordered back into static positions. Peter at the Tennant Street junction and me at the Agnes Street junction. The rioters in the middle. Why, I ask, don't we move in and deal with them? Because the orders from 39 Brigade say that we must contain it and let it burn itself out. Hamstrung again, by some clown sitting behind a desk with not an idea of what is happening on the ground.

We stand there, impotently watching the activities in the middle, stretching further into the evening. At last, the crowds thin out, and in a few moments there is nobody around, just the bright glow from the burning barrier. My skin starts to crawl and the hair stands up on the back of my neck and I'm thinking, *"Christ, the hair really does stand up."*

The C.O. is standing beside me and I scarcely believe his next words: "Tony, take a patrol down and start clearing those barrels out of the middle of the road."

"Did you say clear the barrels, Colonel?" I ask incredulously.

"Don't argue. Do it," says he.

Holy shit! Jesus, you had better be on my side today!

I gather one of my section commanders and three Toms and move away from the security of the Pigs into the now deserted open road. Fright is not the word. Numbness would be nearer, because I know for certain that there is someone out there with a gun.

Ten yards and we are still in one piece. Twenty yards and the sweat is dripping down the inside of my flak jacket. Twenty-five yards and all hell breaks loose. I don't dive for cover, my knees just give out as a burst of fire sends bullets ripping across the wall beside us. I look up to see if anyone has been hit and see Toms scrabbling about on the pavement trying to dig in. My section commander has rolled behind a concrete-filled barrel.

"Go, I'll cover you," says he, and when I pass him I get the idiotic notion that he is covering us with a rubber-bullet gun. No, it can't be true. My ears hurt like hell from the crack of close-passing high-velocity rounds, and everything is moving in slow motion.

The Pigs are just ahead and I can see the Toms in fire positions and the flash as another round is fired down the street. I can see the anxious face of Hookey yelling fire-control orders and the O.C. ducking round a corner as another burst cracks overhead and around my feet.

Somehow, we make it. Twenty-five yards and it was like twenty-five miles. I stumble behind a Pig, turn and see the other Toms bundling into safety. My Cpl. is still behind his barrel and I see to my horror that he really does have a rubber bullet gun. That's like pissing against the wind in this situation.

"O.K., cover Geoff back. Ready, fire."

As the section fires, Geoff leaps to his feet and zigzags back to the Pigs, rounds kicking up the dust on the road beside him and ricocheting off the walls to spin off down the road, embedding themselves in parked cars, doors and other sundry items.

"Where's the fucking C.O.?" I yell at Hookey.

"Gone back to TAC I should think," he yells back.

The noise of the rifles thunders against the walls echoing back against our ears, bouncing away over the roof-tops. The comforting heavy crash of the S.L.R. the chatter of a Thompson and high-pitched crack of the M-16. Having checked that the lads are O.K., I'm trying to get my pulse-rate down and pull together my brain into some co-ordinated action. Anger helps. Anger at that stupid little man. Perhaps it was just as well he did go back to TAC, because the Prots having failed to terminate my Army career, he would have done after I'd hit him. Cunt, cunt, cunt.

I'm still seething as a whoop comes from one of the Toms lying down by the wheel of one of the Pigs.

"I got one of the bastards, I got one."

"Hello 3, this is 33 Lima, one hit over."

"3 Roger out." Cool calm voice of the C.S.M. in stark contrast to my own high-pitched squeal. Peter is also having fun at the other end, so much so that we are getting some of his ricochets.

He, apparently, is also getting some of ours.

The evening is drawing rapidly into night and so taking aim difficult, so now the image-intensifying sight comes into its own. However, we only have one, so the Toms with S.U.I.T. sights fitted are going to be the only others capable of being able to see the targets.

I still have not been able to get permission to move in and take the gunmen out. Apparently because the Northern Ireland Minister himself has taken over control of the situation. Politics, bloody politics. Jesus, now we have civvies running the Army and dictating tactics. Soldiers' lives being gambled for the sake of bloody politics.

A helicopter is now circling overhead and we have him on our Company radio frequency. He has a huge spotlight and by circling well out of the danger zone can light up the whole area that the gunmen are hiding in. We also have an I.T.V. Camera crew with a reporter from *News at Ten*: "You can film, so long as you don't show any faces," says I.

"Fine," says the reporter and we get on with the war.

Lucky he didn't arrive earlier, as we nearly shot one of our own who had appeared in a window between us and the gunmen. My sniper was just about to zap him when I noticed a beret and through the I.W.S. could make out the badge.

"There's one of ours in that house, for fuck's sake don't shoot," I yell, and get straight on the radio.

"Hello 3, this is 33 Lima, there is some clown hanging out of a window, one of ours, and if he doesn't get out he's going to get shot, over."

"3 Roger, out."

I know that the person concerned has heard because the rifle is hastily withdrawn and about ten minutes later the same voice is on the Battalion radio frequency, sitting in the Ops Room at TAC H.Q. Everyone wants to get in on the act. All the fools and idiots who are so bad at basic soldiering techniques that they should never be allowed near an Infantry Battalion. No wonder the blokes have no time for the officers. For sure, if filmed, it could have been a very embarrassing moment.

The battle continues with the pilot of the helicopter telling us where the bodies are being taken, telling us whether or not we have any hits after an exchange of gunfire.

Suddenly a shout from all the platoon and before we know what has happened, they are all firing like crazy, a great cacophony of sound with Hookey and I screaming at them to stop. Which they eventually do. A gunman had leapt into the street and started blazing away like some cowboy out of the movies and was chopped down by God knows how many rounds. Sure as hell there ain't going to be much left to pick up.

A car appears from a side street, lurches, engine screaming, across the road, picks up the dead or wounded man and, tyres squealing, vanishes out of the pool of light away amongst the houses, the Toms firing all the while.

"How is the ammunition, Hookey?" I yell.

"Getting down, we are into our last box."

Our last box of buckshee ammo that is. The stuff we managed to acquire from the previous Battalion, about 400 rounds in all, plus the 10 rounds per man that is issued at the beginning of the tour.

I'm standing alongside Hookey, behind the Pigs trying to figure out the current rate of fire, when a burst of Thompson comes from behind us making long scars in the road between and on either side of us. The O.C. has taken a sideways dive to the pavement and everyone else is looking at us, who have just grasped what's going on, and turn to see Smith firing towards the street that houses one of the biggest U.D.A. clubs in the area.

"Did you get him?"

"I think so, boss, but it's quite hard to see."

"Just keep our backs covered, for Christ's sake, it's what you're here for."

Hookey tells Geoff to go and join Smith on the street corner and as he moves a trail of bullets follow him across the road. Hookey and I are still standing where we were when the last burst came and are by now a little punch-drunk with the noise and the heady charge that comes from announcing another hit on the radio.

Jones, the best shot who is taking out the most gunmen, shouts and rolls over. My heart stops for a second, but he's O.K. The round hit the road just in front of him, throwing chunks of tarmac into his eyes and bouncing off his flash hider. Lucky lad, but he'd better move because the sniper has his position now and next time will be it.

The gunfire is becoming sporadic now as the gunmen begin to get the message and during one of the lulls, a woman comes walking calmly as you like, up to the Pigs from the direction of the city.

"Don't go down the Shankill, love, or you will be likely to get shot."

"Fuck off youse bastard, nobody ever shoots on the Shankill."

With that, she waltzes off past the Pigs and down the road. A hail of bullets stops her dead in her tracks. She freezes, unable to move as the rounds ping around her, and then suddenly she snaps, turns and runs screaming back to the Pigs.

"What did we tell you, stupid cow."

"Christ, you fucking Irish, never listen to a word do you."

The words go straight over her head as she screams in terror, with Hookey eventually slapping her to bring her to her senses again. We send her on her way, physically none the worse for her ordeal but perhaps a little wiser.

The pauses between shots are longer now and it seems that there is perhaps only one gunman left to keep us occupied whilst the others get away. I have been asking Company H.Q. constantly for permission to move in but keep getting the same reply. Stay where you are and only move when we tell you. The whole thing is so frustrating. If we go in now, we can get those that are still alive, the bodies and the weapons, why wait? The pilot of the helicopter has pinpointed the houses that the injured have been taken into and so far we reckon to have zapped about five, but unless we get down there we cannot confirm them and so the whole thing has been a total waste of time. With no confirmation of kills, as in every war, the enemy will deny that they have taken any casualties. It all comes down to political expediency in the end, no confirmed kills and the Prots can continue to be one up on the Catholics. "We may have our little incidents but the Army are really on our side. See, no casualties." As if the whole thing didn't happen.

Silence has descended on the Shankill, lit by the odd remaining street lamps and the flaming barrels still in the middle of the road. A different feeling comes over the place, the tension lifts slightly, an uncanny knowledge that the gunmen have gone, to be confirmed by the helicopter pilot. A scan of the windows and street corners through the I.W.S. does not reveal a thing.

Ten minutes. Twenty minutes. Nothing.

Having conveyed this information to Company H.Q. we finally get the order to move. Not to dig out the bodies as I want but back to Leopold Street, first clearing the barrels out of the way so the traffic can move.

"Did you get that, Hookey?" A nod from him.

"Right, we'll take the Pigs down the outside with the Saracen in the middle leading. Tell your drivers to go straight into the barrels."

"Boss, they could explode, the ones that aren't alight, that is."

"It's a chance we have to take, unless, of course, you want to get out and move them by hand."

So here we go, charging down the road three abreast with the news crew filming away. The Saracen lurches as it hits the barrels and knocks them over to the side of the road. Behind, I can see that, for a heart-stopping moment, one flaming barrel has got stuck under the front of the following Pig, but the driver keeps his nerve and powers straight over the top of it, engine screaming, and the screeching of tortured metal as the steel is dragged along the road. Finally the back wheels bump over it and they are clear.

Fleeting sideways glances down the side streets. Images of bullet-chipped walls, shattered windows and blood on the pavement.

Back at Leopold Street and the place has gone daft. The C.S.M. has bought the whole platoon free beer and we stand there grinning, laughing, excitedly replaying the entire day over and over again like a worn-out record. But it is not over yet. The next stage of the drama takes almost as long as the riot and gun-battle put together. The S.I.B. report.

We have to account for every round fired, produce the empty cases, note the exact time each round was fired, what at, describe it, where was the soldier who fired the round standing, where was the gunman he fired at standing, and on and on and on, into the early hours of the morning. A check is made on each man's magazine, which has been filled to the correct amount he should have in, if he only fired a few rounds as we are claiming. Thank heavens for buckshee rounds, they make life a lot easier. At last the interrogation is over and Hookey and I can now try and get some sleep. After the day's activities we are completely drained and the excitement of the fighting has worn off like a drug, leaving us with mouths like a whore's armpit and a feeling of heavy-headed unreality.

Due to orders from 39 Brigade, we are not allowed into the area for a few hours and must maintain a low profile. Right now, I'm too tired to argue and am thankful just to be able to get my eyes closed for a few hours after a spell of 24 without a break. Too tired to think of the shady dealings going on behind closed doors, of the frantic phone calls by Prot. Leaders to get the Army to stay out of the area so that they can restore order. It makes you wonder what they need us for. At least today, we've taught them that for us the Shankill is just as much a battleground as the Falls or the Ardoyne or the Springfield Road area.

1900 hrs. August 1973

The time
To leave
Draws near.
Am I going
To
Make
It?

I'm looking up at the ceiling of the room I share with Clive thinking of the remaining eight days of the tour and how I'm going to get through them without getting hurt. It is the fear of everyone. Fear of getting zapped in the last few days, after four or five months of boredom and narrow escapes.

Tomorrow the Grenadier Guards advance party arrives and I have to show the platoon commander assigned to me the Shankill in all its glory. So I'm lying here trying to work out how I can best achieve this aim and maintain a low profile. Suddenly self-preservation comes on very strong and I'm not about to go against the survival instinct. It's fairly easy to lose yourself here at the Mill without anybody finding you. Idle thoughts in a moment of relaxation. Since the shoot-out on the Shankill the area has been very quiet, as if the whole thing had never happened, indeed the next day when asking around as to who knew anything about the shooting, the most common answer was: *"Shooting? What shooting? Certainly not on the Shankill!"* This from a bloke who lives not 25 metres from the position a gunman had taken up. Just like the three wise monkeys.

Jesus, what an asylum of a place this is! The trouble is you begin to disbelieve your own eyes and ears after a while and only believe the radio logs, the only thing that can confirm you are here at all – that, and the rifle you carry all day and every day.

Reality is a radio and a rifle. Reality is a milk bottle heading your way. Reality is the sweet sound of expletives rolled out of an Irish mouth at six o'clock in the morning.

Well, can't lie here for much longer otherwise I'll be getting the title "mattress-back", besides which I'm on the Ops Desk in a few minutes to do my stint as duty officer. The lengths of duty go from six to eight hours, sometimes extending *ad infinitum* if there is something on.

From two o'clock in the morning onwards is the best time for me, when I can sit quietly with my own thoughts with just the radio operator for company and drift into a dreamland of peace and gentleness. For an all too brief moment, escape from the stark aggression of everyday living, escape the constant effort to put on a face, and be myself, thinking back to sandy beaches, to the girls and the parties of my adolescence and the innocence, above all the innocence. Secret moments in my head kept safely hidden from the sneers and jokes of my fellow officers. Sitting staring at the map as I have a thousand times before, looking at it as if for the first time, seeing the lines and colours, the names and numbers, pictures gradually forming of old incidents, half-forgotten capsules of life among the dead routine of peace-keeping.

Belfast, I live and breathe you. Belfast, you are etched deep within my soul. Belfast, I have become you and carry the stink of your corpse like a cause.

I'm still at the Ops Desk at ten o'clock in the morning, having had a brief respite for a wash and shave followed by breakfast, when the O.C. comes in with the Grenadiers advance party, to introduce me.

"Tony, this is Bob Nairac who will be assigned to you for the handover period."

I shake hands with a stocky guy with curly black hair, far removed from the normal type of Guards officer you usually meet. I take in the broken nose and cheerful grin and think "Thank God I haven't got one of those guys with a mouthful of marbles." The pleasantries over, he goes off to dump his kit and I'm left alone again with my thoughts and the radio operator gabbling away in my ear.

Just a few more days to go, and the confirmation of that fact written up on the walls of the billets and corridors of the Mill. Everyone trying not to let the anxiety show when on the street, but it wouldn't matter anyway as the Irish know almost to the hour when we are leaving. Secret prayers behind masks of indifference, secret thoughts behind forced laughter.

Soon my private reveries are broken as the Ops Room fills with the Guards officers and N.C.O.s having a quick rundown on the area from the O.C. and a current situation brief from me. The babble of voices makes it difficult to hear the radio so I have to sit with the handset glued to my ear, trying to concentrate and wishing they would all bugger off to the briefing room or the Mess. Having to sit at the Ops Desk for the last twelve hours has put me in a bad mood and I don't particularly want to converse with anyone.

At last the C.S.M. relieves me and I saunter off to the mess for a cup of coffee before making a tour of my blokes who are on guard and stand-by. Clive is there with his opposite number, and Bob, so we fall into the small talk of officers everywhere and rapidly move onto the topic uppermost in all our minds.

Bob is the one with all the questions, insatiable for knowledge, expressing disappointment that his Company is not in the Ardoyne and not convinced when we tell him that we, the Shankill Company, have had more finds and by far the biggest contact of the tour. He is no sooner in the place than he wants to get on the first patrol. It just so happens that I'm due out with one of my sections in an hour's time so he goes away happy, to get his kit together. Clive and I look at each other in disbelief. There's no way we would be so keen to get out there and certainly not at this stage in the tour. In fact, the O.C. had to hound us to get us out into the street. Well, each to his own. Right now I want to stay safe.

Out in the street and Bob is like a foxhound, digging into everything, questioning everything, wanting to cram five months knowledge into one short two-hour patrol. The lads are working well, putting on their best performance to impress the "crap-hats" and the two hours go past quickly, without incident.

It's morning, it's early and it's raining and I don't care about any of it. Today we leave. Today we say goodbye to the grimy streets, the pallid faces, the grinding harsh Irish ghetto slang. Today we say, "Fuck the lot of you, we're going home."

Security is intensified, everyone on the alert for an attack. We pick straws in the platoon to see who will take the last patrol, nobody wishing to tempt fate at this late stage. As for me, for the first time in months I'm singing, nervous at the thought that at the last minute something may go wrong and our tour will be extended for another few months. Not wanting to answer the telephone in the Ops Room in case that's what it is. The Guards are wanting us out of the way so they can get on with it, us wanting to leave them to it. Before we know where we are, the four-ton trucks are assembled and we are on the way down through the early-morning traffic to the docks and the waiting L.S.L.

Heartbeats are faster than normal, eyes more alert than normal, ears hearing the slightest sound above the noise of the vehicle. All the lads trying to be casual, but inside wishing the truck would go a little faster so that we can get aboard that boat.

Into the docks and the breathing becomes a bit easier. Cheers as we see the next load of Guardsmen ready to be transported in.

"Get in there, you suckers."

"Stag on wooden tops."

The yells from the Toms mix with the laughter and obscene gestures, the recipients not looking too happy, wishing to be finished before they have started.

Having got the sleeping arrangements sorted out and left the remainder of the admin to our platoon Sgts, Clive and I wander to the wardroom in search of a drink to break the tension and let out some of the steam of five months of tight control.

There are the other officers in the wardroom and, lo and behold, one of the ship's officers is leaving and so is buying all the drinks up to midday. We need no further encouragement and set to with a will. Shorts of course, and before too long we're getting well and truly pissed. The rest of the day goes by in a blur and before long we are sacked out.

Liverpool. A distant grey blotch in the early morning mist. Liverpool. By the rails, soldiers stand quietly looking at the approaching skyline, the silence broken only by the screeching of sea gulls and the odd shout or obscenity. Liverpool. Home and sanity within our grasp.

Five months have gone since we were last looking at this skyline, then retreating. Five months and it seems a lifetime ago. Standing here in the open air, feeling strange without a flak jacket, radio and rifle, somehow naked.

The C.S.M. joins us by the rail.

"Well young sirs, you've finally got your knees dirty."

Is that what this last five months has been about?

Getting dirty knees?

2: Interlude

2300 hrs. October 1975

It's black outside
And cold.
It's also a long
Way down.
Red On!
Green On!
Out and down.

It seems we've been hanging suspended over the North Sea for weeks. The pilots are sitting dozing whilst the navigator watches the instruments and checks for course corrections. I'm sitting on the jump seat in the back of the cockpit watching the night gradually chase the light out of the sky. Behind us in the belly of the Hercules half the Company are sitting cramped up. Some with their parachutes still on, others sitting on the ramp at the back of the aircraft.

The navigator turns and winks at me.

"Another hour to the southern tip of Norway and then about fifty minutes to the D.Z.," he says above the drone of the four engines. I nod and he carries on scanning the instruments and occasionally making notes. So I'll sit here for another hour and then go and get my parachute back on.

We're off to join the Royal Marines on a N.A.T.O. exercise just south of Oslo. Just one Company from the Battalion, to parachute in as a backup to the sea-borne assault. Most of us will put up with the fear of a night jump onto an unknown D.Z. just to spend a couple of weeks in Norway. The exercise won't last long then it's off to the delights of the town. Still, the first thing we have to do is get there, and once there get on the ground.

Having just come from the Depot after an eighteen-month stint training recruits, I've got quite a few jumps in, but most of the lads in the Battalion don't get the opportunity, therefore every jump is a nightmare. Still, what the hell? All this free travel and an extra pound a day danger money. What more could you ask?

I'm just sitting here talking to myself above the clouds. Mindless silent chit-chat five miles up in the sky. Following behind, two more aircraft. One with the rest of the Company and the other with the heavy drop. A couple of Landrovers and trailers and an anti-tank gun. All bound for a foreign farmer's field in the dead of night. Will the weather be too bad to drop? Where are the trees on the D.Z.? Christ I've forgotten where the R.V. point is! Or have I? I get out my notebook and check it for the thousandth time. Now I've got it. But no doubt will forget again in the next few hours. As always. And as always when everything starts to happen, all the fears drift away with the concentration required for the drop. It's the sitting waiting that screws your insides around and sends you half crazy with worry.

So relax, Clarke. Relax and watch the passing clouds. Relax and think of home. Home. I've almost forgotten where that is. A concrete post-war house tucked away in the pine trees just outside Aldershot. Home. A wife, two children and a dog. My responsibility, my family and yet I hardly know them. When was I last home? Just after coming back from Venice, that's when. The memory makes me smile.

Venice. We had just completed another N.A.T.O. exercise, this time with the crazy Italians. Then it was four days pissing it up wherever we could. Drunken officers stark naked on the tops of restaurant tables dancing and yelling. Getting turfed out of nightclubs at two and three o'clock in the morning where we were trying to sleep. Eventually ending up on the landing of a block of flats huddled together for warmth. The next morning, washing in the railway station and then sitting on the steps shaving, watching Toms racing each other across the canal, dodging the water-buses and gondolas.

Home. This is my home. All these crazy lunatic people are my family. Shit, I don't know any more and right now I really don't care.

I drift out of my daydream. Back to the roar of the engines and smell of Avtur and pressurisation. The loadmaster is nudging me and pointing to the rear. Suddenly my guts start to feel weaker and the heart beats a little faster. It's time to go back and start getting organised for the drop. Shit, I hate this part.

Oh well. Haul myself off the seat and climb down the steps from the cockpit into the rear of the aircraft. The engine note changes and the plane starts to descend. As it goes down through the clouds there is some turbulence. The conditions in the back are hardly what you'd call first-class; tourist class would be a positive luxury compared to this shambles. Men and equipment everywhere. All having to clamber over each other. I find my place and struggle into the harness, helped by the guys on either side of me. Having got it fastened and my tin helmet on I sit sweating, sandwiched between two burly soldiers. Container clamped between my knees with the leg strap attached and the quick release fastened to the right hip.

Check and double check. Where the hell is my static line? O.K., breathe again. I've found it. Get it where it should be Clarke, over the left shoulder. Well done!

The loadmaster struggles down the aisle over the packs and knees checking the equipment. By now the aircraft has descended to just above dropping height. As soon as we get to Oslo Fjord, we descend as low as possible then pop up just prior to dropping. The ride is quite rough now and every now and then somebody throws up, the smell wafting around mixing with the Avtur and sweat and other human smells. What a great way to spend an evening.

This bouncing nightmare ride continues for about twenty minutes and then it comes. The loadmaster signals to stand up and fit equipment. The weight of the two parachutes is bearable when seated, but once standing the tight straps cut into my shoulders. The helmet feels like a clamp around my head and the sweat runs in rivulets down into my eyes. I have to keep blinking. For the first time I'm wearing contact lenses for a drop. Why I don't know, as it will be pitch black out there and I won't be able to see anyway.

Struggle to turn around in the tight confines of the aircraft and hook up the container. All eighty pounds of it. There is now one hundred and thirty pounds of dead weight slung around my shoulders, and no way of resting it properly.

Forget the discomfort; just don't forget to hook up. I would look silly going out with my static line still hung over my shoulder.

For God's sake get those doors open is the internal scream. Some of the smaller lads are nearly on their knees, bowed down by the weight of the equipment. As if hearing us, the lights go out in the cabin to be replaced by a dull red glow. This is to get our eyes used to the dark, so that once on the ground we will be able to see as best we can. The doors are opened and the welcome blast of cold air rushes in, cooling the sweat on our faces. Everybody gulps in the air. Outside it is pitch black. Over in the distance, the lights of a village eight hundred feet below. Just above the aircraft, clouds whip past. We are right on the borderline of whether to jump or not.

There is the telltale straightening of the aircraft and the slight change in attitude that tells us we're on the run-in. The tension increases. Christ, the straps are tearing my shoulders off.

The loadmaster shakes his head and waves his arms. No drop this time around. The pilot has missed the run-in. Good old "crab-air", never reliable, always fucking us about. You can hear the groans and moans above the sound of the engines and the rushing air. Being number three in the stick I can look out of the door and see the empty blackness of the D.Z. slip away beneath us. The aircraft banks and begins the next circuit. They haven't told us to sit down again so presumably the jump is still on. If we don't go this time a little R.A.F. pilot is going to be hung up by his balls.

Circuit completed and we are lining up again. This time the red light comes on. Ten seconds to go. The green flashes and suddenly we're moving. Straight out into that black night.

I've made a good exit. It's the first thing that crosses my mind as I plummet down in the night. There is a tug as the static line pulls the parachute out, then once free of its bag it whips overhead and once again there is the sensation of being on a big swing until the canopy opens and there is silence. Check for twists. None. Good. Check for anybody else close by and then drop the container. The hooks snap open and the container drops away on its length of nylon rope to dangle nearly twenty feet below.

I've drifted clear of the main stick. Away to the left two idiots have got themselves tangled and there is much cursing and swearing carrying quite a long way in the night. All around shadows of canopies drifting down towards the Norwegian countryside.

All very pretty, I think, looking around drifting in the blackness. Then with a start I remember the sodding ground coming up at sixteen feet per second to smash a bone or two.

Look down and see a black mass. The realisation of the tree reaching out to grab me was almost too late. Tuck legs up. Arms in front of my face and wait for the crash.

The container catches first and then I smash straight into the topmost branches. The parachute collapses and I'm falling through the tree bouncing off branches and eventually come to rest, caught up by the harness.

Here in the trees the darkness is total. The silence complete. I wonder if I've broken anything? Forget the exercise, think of my poor battered body. I feel bruised but everything moves as it should do. Thank Christ for that. Breathe a sigh of relief and try and get out of this mess. Question. How far up am I? There is no way of knowing. The only thing to do is pull the reserve and try and climb down the rigging lines. I pull the handle and let the parachute fall out of its bag and down to the ground. The next thing is to get out of this harness without dropping straight out of the tree. This could be fun. Grab the rigging lines over my head with one hand then turn and hit the buckle with the other.

I've never felt such an idiot in my life. The distance to the ground is approximately six inches. Thank fuck there is nobody watching.

I must have fallen from the top to the bottom to be held just before hitting the ground. Lucky. Now where's my container? Follow the rope and it leads me straight to a stream. The rope disappears. Great. When I finally get the container out of the stream and unwrapped, all my clothes are wet through. With the temperature near freezing point and a light drizzle falling, it's going to be one of these fun exercises.

"Anybody there?" A voice in the darkness, to shake me out of my self-pity.

"Lt. Clarke over here. Who's that?"

"Leighton. There's a couple of others. I'll bring them over."

The whispered Geordie voice stopped and there was rustling as he moved away to collect the others. I pick up my bergen, get it onto my shoulders having first strapped my belt pouches on, then with rifle nestled in the crook of my arm, wait. It's then that I realise I've lost my contact lenses. Boy what a night this is. Movement in the bushes.

"Over here lads!" a whispered command.

A thud. A curse. A stifled laugh and there are three shadows in front of me.

"Right. Follow me. Keep close until we get out of the trees." A few paces through the trees and I can see the lighter area that shows where the D.Z. is. Struggle through the undergrowth a little further and then we're sitting on the ground on the edge of the wood whilst I take stock.

"There's a couple more lads over there, boss. Shall I get them?" He goes off taking his rifle but leaving his pack. That gives me time to figure out the direction of the R.V. An unknown point in a strange land at night in the rain. It seems as if it's been raining all my life. Leighton returns with half a dozen blokes and we set off for the D.Z., me leading and hoping I've got it right.

Fifteen minutes of stumbling over ploughed fields and tracks and then a click from just in front.

"Halt! Hands up." The RV sentry. We go through the procedure, then split up to find our platoon areas.

"Finally made it, boss? What took you so long?" Sgt. Denny lying on the sodden ground. No doubt he is grinning as usual, if I could see his face in the dark.

"No bones broken, I trust?"

"No. Just landed in trees, lost my contact lenses and dropped my bergen in a stream." It's difficult to roar with laughter without making a lot of noise but he manages it.

"Now boss, don't crack." The banter continues in whispers. The rain continuing to soak everything. Toms lying on the wet ground, helmets on the backs of their heads, chins resting on rifle butts, each alone in their own thoughts.

"Lt. Clarke, O.C. wants you for a briefing." I nod at my radio op. and together we make our way over to the O Group. The other platoon commanders are there and we grin at each other in the pool of dull light from a couple of torches set up beneath a bivvy. The O.C. looks slightly comical sat in all his kit, beret on back of head, face smeared with camouflage cream. We all squash together and sit expectantly with waterproofed maps and notebooks at the ready.

"Orders." The well-remembered word signifying the start of the briefing. Heads down. Look in.

"We've been sitting here for fucking hours. What's going on?"

"Shut up Smith. Why can't you do as you're told. Idiot." He's got a point though. What the fuck are we waiting for? According to the orders, once we made it to the Form-up Point it would only be a few minutes before the attack went in. I get up and crawl over to where the O.C. is slumped against a tree shivering.

"What's the hold-up, Major?"

"The Marines haven't got themselves into position yet."

"When do they expect to be there?"

He gives me a sidelong look and shrugs. "From what I can make out on the Battalion radio net, they are nowhere near ready. Rest assured it will be hours."

Rest assured he says. The temperature is dropping, we have no winter warfare kit, everyone is soaking wet and freezing and the bloody Marines are pissing about because they can't read a fucking map.

Thinking all this while I crawl back down the tree lined track to where my platoon, as advanced party, are hidden in the bushes and trees getting colder and colder. It would be very easy for a few of them to give up. What am I saying? The constant rain, which has now stopped thank God, must have penetrated my brain.

"Sgt. Denny?"

"Yes boss. Over here."

"It's going to be a very long night. We'd better get everybody closed up. That way they might keep each other warm."

"Already done boss."

"Clever shit. Seems like the Marines are still wandering Norway trying to find the airfield."

"Wouldn't surprise me, they spend so much time at sea the salt water must rust their brains away."

The conversation carries on in low tones, whiling the time away thinking this is a very strange way to earn a living. At least here in the cover of the trees we're saved from the wind.

"Let one man per section brew up under cover of a poncho."

"Good idea." He crawls over to the section commanders and soon there is the telltale smell of hexamine. We wouldn't do it in action, but I've reasoned that tonight there is a case for it. It's either get some hot drink inside some of these guys or suffer the consequences of exposure. The O.C. better agree. If he finds out. Would be interesting if the Marines suddenly decided they were ready. No chance. I tell myself. And hope I'm right.

"Here boss. Get some of this down inside you!"

"Cheers. Any problems?"

"Not yet. The brew really helped."

"I just hope they realise they can't do this in South Armagh."

"I don't reckon it's going to be that cold in South Armagh."

"You're right." Somewhere out there are Marines wandering around looking for an airfield and lots of little part-time Norwegian soldiers waiting to be attacked. We know where the Norwegians are but nobody knows where the dumb Marines are. To cap it all, it's just started to snow very lightly. Already there is a thin coating of the white stuff all over the trees, the ground and us. Marvellous. Why couldn't it wait for Christmas.

Away in the distance there is the sound of gunfire. After the initial stir of interest everyone settles down again.

"Seems as if they have started to get themselves together."

"Doubt it. Probably walking into their own ambush."

"Why don't you get some kip, boss. I'll wake you in an hour."

It makes sense. So I pull my poncho over myself and try and sleep. It's incredible. When you're really tired you can sleep anywhere. A skill learned in Belfast in '73. Fitful slumber, to wake with aching bones and a lightheaded feeling. Having woken me from my short sleep, Sgt. Denny nods off supported by the trunk of a pine tree.

It's now nearly four o'clock in the morning and the light is slowly beginning to filter through the darkness, casting strange shadows on the landscape.

I must have dozed off, because the next thing I know is that my radio operator is shaking me.

"Message from One sir. Ready to move in ten minutes."

"Right. Relay to the sections."

"I've done that." Boy, I'd better get a grip of things.

"Wake up Jimmy. Moving in ten minutes."

"I heard."

Suddenly there is activity all around. The rustle and clinking of men getting their equipment together. Low murmurs, purposeful whispers and the air of excitement that chases away the cold and the tiredness. For the first time we can see the countryside in the light of dawn.

"Looks like fucking Sennybridge."

"Perhaps we are in fucking Sennybridge."

"If we are, then I'm going down to Sarah Siddons tonight."

"You're just wishful thinking, cunt. There's no big Liz in this country."

"Bet I find one."

"You're just looking to get poxed up, you prick." And so on. The sound of Toms coming alive.

"Cut the crap. Let's go. Make sure that radio is on Smith."

"O.K. That's it. The end. Finish."

"Hoorah." Chorus of cheers from the band of filthy wet smelly soldiers.

"Thank fuck for that. Let's get down to the serious business of drinking and whoring."

"What would you know about women, Anson?" The baby-faced Tom colours slightly.

"Oh piss off!" Jeers and catcalls. Now that the exercise is over, suddenly the tiredest Tom comes alive and shows remarkable alacrity, especially when it comes to climbing into the back of a four-ton vehicle. Four days of seeking the fleshpots of Oslo coming up. Firstly we have to find the camp. It takes two hours to get there. Once there the enthusiasm and cheerfulness disappear as we stare at accommodation.

What a joke.

It is a tented camp. Round dark-green canvas obscenities with duckboards on the muddy ground and a wood fire in the middle belching out smoke, making the eyes stream and everything smell. These Marines sure know how to fuck things up.

The platoon commander's tent is like something out of films about the Khyber Pass. A white ridge tent with high walls and ties for the flaps.

"Fuck this. Let's find the Mess." So off Pete and I go in search of the Officers Mess. It's a long walk but we find it eventually. The next ten minutes is spent wandering around the corridors.

"Hey Tone, look at the names on these doors. Sgt. Murphy, W.O.2 Grant, Sgt. Macbain, etc. What do the little shits think they are playing at. Sticking all their N.C.O.s into the Mess with no room even for the O.C."

"Come on, let's find someone. Fucking cabbage-heads. Couldn't organise a piss-up in a brewery. Bastards." There's a passing Sgt.

"Sgt., who's in charge of the accommodation here?"

"Who wants to know?"

"Put a sir on the end of that and answer the question. Just who do you think you're talking to?"

"I beg your pardon, sir. I am."

"Then where are our rooms?"

"You don't have any." There is a smirk on his face that is going to get wiped off with the butt of my rifle if he's not careful.

"Really. Then let me put it to you this way. My Company

Commander better have a room by the time he arrives or the fucking shit is going to hit the fan so hard it'll take those stripes straight off your arm. Do I make myself perfectly clear?"

"Yes sir." He disappears off and Pete and I are just leaving when our Norwegian Captain friend arrives.

"Are you staying here?"

"No. It seems we haven't been allocated rooms."

"Then come and stay with me at my house. I'll bring you in every morning. But not tonight. I have arranged a party with twelve lovely girls. Very intelligent and very pretty. Can you bring twelve people?"

"No problem. Where is it?" He gives us the address of a hotel in Oslo and we go off to sort the soldiers out in a reasonable frame of mind. In order to get twelve people some of the Marines are going to have to come. We ask a few but all we get is the excuse that they are not allowed to leave camp. Fucking crap-hats. Professionally inept and social dwarfs. Pete and I then approach our senior N.C.O.s all of whom are only too pleased to go along.

Once the admin is out of the way, the O.C. piles us all into a couple of open Landrovers and off to Oslo we go. Twelve paratroopers looking for a screw. Twelve overgrown juveniles off to the fleshpots like kids just let out of school for the day. Who cares. Let's enjoy it. We'll eat the elk steaks, drink the lager with aquavit chasers. Get pissed and then try and lay a willing Norwegian girl.

Tomorrow we could get killed.

3: Rain and Rubber Ducks

1130 hrs. April 1976

Bright sunlit morning
Reflecting off whitewashed walls
Shining off wire mesh
Dazzling across wrinkly tin
Blocked by camouflage netting.

The clatter of the helicopter comes clearly through the afternoon skies, and the nervous chatter increases a little.

"Helipad, this is Ops Room, chopper in two minutes."

"O.K." I reply, "Where's the O.C?"

"Just coming," says the dismembered voice through the intercom.

Our first patrol as a platoon on our first day here at Crossmaglen and the O.C. wants to come out to have a look at the border. Just the sort of thing I can do without on this the first time in action with my new platoon. The N.C.O.s came out with me on the advance party, so we've been here a week trying to learn the ground and get as much information as possible, now I want a shake-down to make sure everyone is working as per training and that there are no major worries.

"What's the O.C. coming out for, boss?" This from one of the section commanders.

"He wants to see the area."

"Then why doesn't he go with some other bugger?"

The complaining continues and I check my equipment for the fiftieth time. Map, compass, belt and pouches, codes, personality check-list, stolen car list, ammunition, rifle and lastly my radio op to see whether he has everything.

"All set, Tony?" the O.C. creeping up on me.

"No problems. If you stay with Cpl. Menzies' patrol it will give them less to aim at."

"Fine."

The clatter of the Wessex becomes deafening as it swoops over the top of the police station and round the football pitch to descend onto the helipad. As it touches down we race out and throw our kit in, clambering after it. The shorter the turn-around the better, and within a few seconds we are airborne and moving tactically along at low level, swinging round trees and hills, dropping into little gullies, dodging power lines and telephone wires.

We are moving down towards Cullaville right on the border with the Republic. The Wessex swings round in a tight turn, drops, flares and touches on the soggy turf. As soon as the wheels touch we are off and running. Guns into fire positions, my section commanders and I showing them the route. There's no time to notice the tight feeling in your stomach, or the nervous playing with the safety catch.

"O.K. Cpl. Menzies, move off."

I look over to the right and see the third patrol in position on the side of a small hill, to give cover to our two patrols that will be moving. Bill, Cpl. Menzies, is moving slowly away towards the road. First objective, a V.C.P. on the Crossmaglen to Cullaville Road.

"Right lads, let's go."

We follow, fight our way through the blackthorn hedge and position ourselves on the road. It's an eerie feeling standing there knowing that there are hidden pairs of eyes watching us and logging every move we make for future reference.

Having talked about it in the Mess the night before, we reckon that the chances of getting hit on the first day are pretty small, because the opposition don't know how we are going to operate, and, being far more professional than the cowboys in Belfast, they will not do anything until they are sure of a kill.

Pleasant thoughts on the ground, everything looking so innocent with the sun shining on the green fields, the gentle breeze swaying the trees, the sounds of the birds.

Hello, a car.

Bill flags him down and suddenly the old familiar routine of the V.C.P. comes flooding back and I am no longer unsure of my ability and begin to relax.

"11 Roger out."

Without me being aware, the radio op has given a car check and received the reply. Well at least someone is thinking, if not me. The O.C. is deep in conversation with the driver of the car, being about as subtle as a pork pie in a synagogue.

"You mean to tell me you don't know what goes on around here," he is saying to a fairly elderly Irishman who looks like an ordinary farmer to me. "Come now, you must know what's going on."

Well, he's stubborn, that's for sure, but the old boy is not about to say a thing even if he does know what's going on. The lads are looking bored with the questioning, and eventually the O.C. lets the guy go.

Ten minutes we've been on this V.C.P. - that's too long, so as soon as the car has gone we are up and moving. Back through the hedge, up to the covering patrol, and on over the fields. This is just a short patrol so we are moving back towards the base, checking things as we go.

Little crofts are tucked into the sides of the hills, their land extending to a few acres of not very good soil. Cullaville itself consists of a small housing estate, the odd shop and a few other houses dotted on the side of the Concession Road. This is a road that cuts across the apex of the triangle of land south of Crossmaglen and allows for the people from the South to cut across Northern Irish territory without having to go through the customs' procedure. That's a laugh. Most of the customs' posts have been blown up, so it is easy for anyone wanting to enter the U.K. to stroll across the border, climb on a ferry and go to England. What a joke.

There is one thing about being here, at least the air is fresh and it's good to feel the earth beneath your feet instead of hard tarmac and paving stones. If only we didn't have to fight. Still, it's the job you volunteered for, Clarke, so you can just get on with it. Forget home and comfort, think nasty. Think bombs and bullets. Think death.

My patrol closes up on Bill's, which is down in a cover position for the other patrol now moving up towards us. The O.C. has the map out and is staring at it in confusion.

"I'm just trying to pinpoint exactly where we are, Tony."

"Just there," says I, leaning over his shoulder and displaying my teeth in a grin to Bill.

"Oh yes, of course, fine, thank you."

"I think we should start moving back to the base Major, we've been out for a couple of hours now and the next patrol is due out soon."

"Right, let's go."

Fighting through the blackthorn is the most difficult way of moving across country, but in this part of the world it is the safest way to travel. By making our own holes we lessen the risk of running into a booby trap, many of which have been planted on gateposts, in drainage culverts under roads, and so on. No vehicles are allowed on the roads down here, so all movement is either on foot or by helicopter. The place is a minefield, covered with homemade landmines, just waiting for the opportunity to be detonated under a patrol.

What a delightful part of the world to spend a summer. Who would think that this is part of the British Isles? Here we are walking around with three machine guns, two M79 grenade launchers, a personal rifle and enough ammunition to have a fair-size war all on our own. All the weapons are cocked and waiting for the off. Well, you wanted excitement Clarke, you are getting it. At least the same rules don't necessarily apply down here as they do in Belfast, or at least people are willing to turn a blind eye to any infringements of the letter of the yellow card. Sure as hell, if I see some bastard with a gun, I'm not about to ask him to surrender. Shoot first, then ask questions after. No way am I going to take any chances at all. Crossmaglen. All through my service, this place has figured prominently in the news. That it's a death-trap is in no doubt, but it is surprising to find out just how small the town is. In fact, to spend a two-hour foot patrol in it is hard to do, without crossing your path a few times.

"Fuck, fuck, fuck. Cunting thing."

Shaken out of my reverie by the dulcet tones of Smith my radio op getting stuck in the blackthorn and ripping his denims open.

"Don't worry, Smith, you'll get used to patching those up by the end of the tour."

He just glares and mumbles away to himself whilst the others behind laugh. I managed to scrounge some gloves off the departing Royal Scots, which at least protect the hands from the vicious thorns. However, the gloves are for issue to winter-tour troops only and so far every effort to get some for us have failed. Good old bureaucratic red tape as usual. Perhaps one of the civil servants who makes these decisions should be made to do a four-month tour. That would soon change his mind.

We get Smith disentangled from the hedge and move into fire positions to cover the other patrols up and past us. I can see Jones on the gun, crawling into a good place, carefully setting the gun up and hear the sliding click as he cocks it.

Out with the map and check the surrounding countryside. I see that when we get to the top of the hill in front of us, we should be able to see straight across to the base. I don't know if the word base is a good description, it's more like a fortress, bristling with OPs, each with a machine-gun and plenty of ammunition, covered over with wire mesh so that mortar bombs or grenades don't penetrate. The whole thing is sandbagged and with super-thick walls to minimise the effect of any blast. An old provincial police station built to house a few local constables; it is now the home for over one hundred and thirty men in cramped conditions. The only lifeline, the helicopters that fly in the food and patrols, and fly out the rubbish and more patrols.

The Battalion has one other Company in a border base at Forkhill over to the east of us, nestling on the other side of a spur of the mountain I can see rising darkly out of the green land. Smith nudges me.

"Company H.Q. want to know our location, sir."

I give it to him to send in code and go back to planning the next part of the route on the map and on the ground. The other two patrols are getting closer and will be with us in a few minutes. So I have time just to look around a little more.

The problem with crossing the fields is that they are all so small, so no sooner have you fought your way through one bloody hedge than another is there before you. We are getting too far away from the road and will have to swing to the west so that we can put another V.C.P. on before going back in. I wish I didn't have to keep looking at the map; still, given time, I'll get to know the area like the back of my hand and won't have to rely solely on the map.

"Come on, you lot, get your arses up here. I want to get to the top of the hill and have a look-see."

"Which section's on stag first, when we get back, boss?"

"I think you'll find that Jimmy has already figured it all out and has the whole thing under control."

"Look at that, for fuck's sake."

The O.C. has got himself entangled in the blackthorn and emerges with as much dignity as he can muster. He is tall with eyes that pop out, giving him the look of a frog and the Toms the chance to coin the nickname "Rivet", being the noise a frog makes. So that's all you can hear for the next few minutes.

"Rivet, rivet! Rivet, rivet!"

Whether he knows that it is aimed at him, I've no way of telling but he certainly has given no indication that he knows. This, of course, allows the Toms to do it mercilessly.

Finally, the other patrols arrive and move into position and I can now go on up to the top of the hill and see just where we are. I struggle through another blackthorn hedge cursing silently. Fall over, get to my feet and carry on.

Suddenly a loud explosion rips the air from the direction of the base, followed rapidly by another and then the rippling crack of machine-gun and rifle fire. Holy shit, they've done it. The bastards have done it. I leap forward, Bill running with me. Turning to yell, I can see the O.C. standing stock-still, the shock keeping his feet rooted to the ground. My yell has penetrated and everyone is moving.

Through the next blackthorn panting with exertion, heart hammering, shaking with nerves, and there is the base a thousand metres ahead with a pall of smoke hanging over it and the gunfire echoing across the fields. We must get to a road and put a V.C.P. on and see if we can get the bastards before they get back across the border.

"Come on you cunts, get your butts up here," I yell, running down a track that I hope will lead to the Crossmaglen and Cullaville road. All caution is thrown to the wind in the confusion of the moment. Got to block the road. There it is.

"Smith, over here with the radio. Jones, get the gun up there. Bill, your patrol back up the road. Where's Cpl. Edge?" Where the hell is he? Then I see him just on the brow of a small hill overlooking the road.

"Smith, tell Cpl. Edge to stay where he is and cover us." The O.C. comes racing up, white-faced.

"Smith, a message to One. Tell them that we are blocking the Cullaville road."

Before the O.C. can say anything a message comes through that a rocket or two were fired at a Wessex coming in to land, followed by a small-arms attack on the base itself. The O.C. is hopping up and down wanting to know the full details and I'm trying to get him away from the radio so that the 2I.C., who is in command at the base at the moment, can get on with the job of putting in a counter attack. There is nothing we can do from here except block off the road and hope we catch someone. I'm having my doubts, because looking at the map the easiest way to the border is down the Dundalk road, which is a thousand metres over to our east. Shit, shit, shit.

The firing dies away and the silence stretches on as if nothing had happened. It's weird and a little spooky. Nothing has changed, the trees are still there, the clouds are drifting by and the sun is still shining. If it wasn't for the radio traffic and the now dispersing black smoke, there would be no reason to think that this wasn't an ordinary day. What am I saying? It is an ordinary day in this part of the world!

The only car on the road is a Cortina heading at a leisurely pace down towards us, stopping dutifully when signalled.

"All right, out of the car, hands in the air and you too, darling."

"Now open the boot and bonnet, slowly."

The short, black-haired man does just that and the curvy girl he has with him stands hands on hips sneering at us.

"Where were you when that little fracas started?" I ask him.

"And what might that be?" says he, calm as you like. It's difficult not to take a swing at him. For all we know there might be dead bodies littered all over town.

"Are you trying to tell me that you didn't hear the explosions and rifle-fire, sunbeam?"

"Come to think of it, I did hear a noise, didn't you darlin'?"

"Well?"

"Nothin' to do with me, I'm just drivin' through with me girl-friend."

"Of course you were."

We go through the routine of P. Check and Vehicle Check and find that although there is nothing concrete on the bloke, he is definitely a suspect and on file in the Int. section back at Crossmaglen. The search takes quite a long time, the whole car having a thorough going over but with the result we expect. Zero. Zilch. Nothing. The O.C. has taken over talking to our hard-of-hearing Irish friend and I check back and find out what is happening at the base. It has been about fifteen minutes now since the firing ceased, so any hope of catching the perpetrators is gone. We cannot keep the two suspects any longer so the O.C. decides to lift the V.C.P. and go back in, sweeping through the woods and waste ground between us and the base. This could be fun. The chance of anyone still being around is remote, but then we had thought getting zapped on the first day was remote.

Oh well, take a deep breath, collect the patrols together and let's go.

"Hello 1, this is 11, we are approaching the rear of your location and will be in view in two minutes, over."

"1 Roger out."

I don't want some trigger-happy Tom with the excitement of combat still on him, giving me a belt of 7.62mm rounds as soon as I show my face beyond the next hedge. No doubt there are a couple up in the OPs just itching to shoot at anything in sight. Let's just stay here a minute, give plenty of time for the message to get through. Beyond the hedge, I can see the base and the helipad with the stricken Wessex standing there, its rotor blades drooping as if feeling the pain of the rounds.

Right, out into the open and thank the Lord, no rounds are flying our way. Leaving one patrol to cover our backs we move down the football pitch towards the back gate, which hopefully will have someone there to open it. Passing the Wessex, the colander effect of the bullets is plainly visible and it is also obvious that if there had been a full load of soldiers on board, a large proportion of them would either be dead or badly injured. This time we were very lucky.

"Bill, leave three men to cover the other patrol back in, then everybody into the briefing room in ten minutes."

"O.K. boss."

The O.C. has raced off to the Ops Room to find out what happened and I'm off to the bog because my guts are playing up. There isn't room to swing a cat in the base, so you have to thread your way past the scaffolding of the OPs and the accommodation that has been built into what was the courtyard of the police station.

"Hey, Tony, you missed all the fun," John, one of the platoon commanders, is coming towards me grinning from ear to ear. "It was great."

"That I will take your word about. What happened?"

"We were waiting by the gate for the chopper which had just taken out my platoon sergeant's half. As it was coming in to land they fired an R.P.G.7 at it. The pilot and crew member saw it coming and managed to pull up in time, then he dumped it and jumped straight out of the cockpit. There was a lot of shooting going on so I took my patrol out and skirmished across to the bank on the other side of the helipad with the OP covering with the gun. They must have been a bit shocked by the speed of the reaction because when we got there they had gone."

"Where did the shots come from?"

"The waste ground by the hall. They must have had a car waiting and gone straight down the Dundalk road to the border. I think we may have hit one."

"Wishful thinking."

"You wait, there'll be some funeral notice in the next few days," he says.

"No way," and with that we part company, him going off on patrol, me to do my thing.

There is nothing like a contact to get the tour off to a good start, providing, that is, that none of ours are killed. Hey-ho, such is war.

"Cor, it was fucking great mate. You should have seen sarge giving them fucking rooty-toot. Great mate, great." The war stories are starting already. Let's hope you get to tell them in Aldershot.

The base here at Crossmaglen just has to be the biggest tactical farce of the whole Northern Ireland thing. It is situated in a pocket of the North surrounded on three sides by the border with the Republic, and the entire population of the district, with the exception of a couple of Prots, are Catholic, anti-British, pro-I.R.A. and a law unto themselves. Bandit country, the media have called it and it's not a bad label. The law, as such, does not apply here. Court summonses are ignored, taxes and bills unpaid, but they draw the dole even though a lot go off to the South to work. Then there is the Army base, sitting near the centre of town just asking for trouble. I would love to meet the lunatic who decided to set up a base here; he must have at least three heads.

The Ops Room is chaos, so I slip quietly by and go on up to what we laughingly call the "Mess". It is a couple of tiny rooms shared by the officers and senior N.C.O.s and if we were all to get in them at once, it would be standing room only. I've managed to get a bunk of my own, a room 7ft long by about 5ft deep. Just enough to get a bed and a drawer unit into. It must have been a broom-cupboard at one time. Anyway, at least I can have some privacy sometimes, being the senior platoon commander and all that.

The pilot and crew member of the chopper are sitting in the Mess looking a little pale and chattering away like crazy. Well, these R.A.F. blokes don't expect this sort of thing to happen to them. I think I'll leave them to it. I really can't stand war stories, especially on this first day. There is plenty of time for all that, let's get through the tour first and have the lengthy post-mortem in the comfort of Aldershot.

Down in the briefing room, my platoon staff and I are discussing the arrangements for the next week.

"We are going to be stretched for manpower, because not only do we have the OPs to man but also a town patrol and the admin duties to perform. The C.S.M. wants the whole camp cleaned up and painted so that it at least looks presentable." My platoon sergeant giving the N.C.O.s the good news. There's more.

"Boss, I've got you down to take out the first town patrol seeing as you know the area so well."

"Cheers mate, I didn't think you would be sitting idly by whilst we were working."

He grins and utters those immortal words: "Quack. Quack." The rubber duck has followed us.

"O.K., I'll take Bill's patrol with me and you can put the others on stand-by."

Cpl. Menzies groans and rolls his eyes heavenwards.

"Why didn't we get the country patrols first, boss?"

"Because it will give us a chance to go through all the Int. reports and the personality files. I want the whole platoon genned up on all there is to know about this place. Anyway, going out tonight will give us a chance to have a good look around the hall and see if we can figure out a fire position."

"What time, boss?"

"In here at 1800 hrs."

"O.K., if you start getting your lads sorted out now, the OPs are manned, and I'll stick the rota and programme up in the stand-by room."

With that last word from my Sgt. the meeting breaks up and we go through to the Ops Room to see what is going on. The 2I.C. is still at the desk fighting off the phone calls from TAC wanting to know what had been happening. He apparently switched the radio off after giving the initial contact and didn't put it back on until he was ready to give a full report. The constant questions that come over the air from TAC H.Q. in a contact situation are a pain and make trying to concentrate on the problem impossible. However, they are not very pleased and are in the process of giving him an earful. All of which goes straight over his head. He's too old to be messed about with and when this tour is finished is leaving the Army anyway, so doesn't give a damn what he says or to whom. A man after my own heart.

"Fucking TAC, can't send us anything to get this chopper out of here until tomorrow."

"What's up with it?" I ask casually.

"It has a suspected ruptured fuel line to one of the engines where the tail fin of the rocket caught it and the pilot says he won't fly it out unless he has both engines working."

Very inconvenient. While that thing sits there, no other helicopters can get in without landing in the open on the playing field.

"Can't they get somebody down here to fix it, or at least give an opinion?"

"Yes, some mechanic is coming."

Well, if he is going to be out there fixing it that will mean lights and a guard all night. The lads will be happy. At least there is good protection with the guns up in the OPs.

"Come on boss, I'll make us a brew." So Denny, my Sergeant, and I go. Leaving the 2I.C. storming away on the phone.

The square of Crossmaglen, only fifty metres down from the base, is getting darker with the fading light, the surrounding grey buildings throwing long shadows over the rough tarmac of the streets, vanishing into the pools of yellow light from weak street lights. This has been the last conscious sight that many soldiers have had, and no doubt will be for many more to come.

It's quiet with the only sound coming from the odd cars driving through. The bars are filling up but not as noisily as you would expect. Quiet men, sipping quiet pints in quiet corners. The look of distrust written all over them. Up on the hill to the east of the town the church stands blackly in the dusk, exuding a menace that is hard to define. If you aren't agnostic already, a trip to Northern Ireland will certainly make you one. How many evils have been committed in this country in the name of religion? How many have been martyred to a senseless cause? The shadows don't answer and the men can't.

We patrol quietly, slowly and stealthily. Although we are not going to be using flak jackets for the country patrols, it is ordered that we wear them in the town. They take a bit of getting used to, as they are heavy and unyielding. It is during these first patrols that we find out which of the lads are going to need some rapid knocking into shape. Already there are a couple who sound like falling tins as they run, equipment rattling and clanking. Bill is getting more furious by the minute and, for sure, some unlucky Tom is going to get panned when we get back.

It is very lonely out here, the whole atmosphere is charged with hatred and I can feel eyes watching us from behind curtained windows and hedgerows. We are right in the heart of their country and they only have to bide their time before zapping us again. The worst thing is just having to wait for it to happen without being able to do a thing about it. Only our instincts and training are going to save us and sometimes that is not enough.

"Right, out of the car, bonnet and boot open, please." Bill has stopped a car, so the check and P. Check procedure is gone through again.

"Where are you from and where are you going?"

"Just come from down the road and I'm going up there." Really helpful these people.

"Now let's try that again, shall we? I'm going to ask you where you come from and where you are going to, and you are going to tell me. Exactly. O.K.?"

"I come from my house and I'm going to the pub."

"Well, we're getting there aren't we? Now where do you live?"

He finally tells us and clears out on the P. Check. Pity. There are times when I really would like to have the powers that the South African Police have, then perhaps we would get a bit of co-operation instead of being messed about all the time. They know there is nothing much we can do and anyway, they've been through it countless times with different units so it's just another day to them.

He gets back into his battered wreck of a car and drives off, the raucous sound of the broken exhaust echoing back off the walls. There is nothing going on, the town is quiet as if lying in wait to see what reaction they have sparked by the helicopter incident.

I get the feeling of being one of those shooting-gallery targets that go round on a conveyor belt, endlessly waiting for someone to knock it down. Trouble is if you get knocked down here, you don't get up. Turn right at the next corner, tell the OP that we are moving around the waste area by the hall. This is where I suspected that the rocket was fired from, so we'll just take a look around for any evidence.

"Boss, there's a hole in the glass in that top window and another through the netting covering it."

Bill's voice low and whispered. I look up and see that there is a flight of steps leading up. Creep up, checking for trip-wires as I go and find an open door at the top leading into a large room running the width of the hall and about twenty feet deep. The window in question has a good view of the helipad and so could have been the place for the rifles to have been fired from, but because of the back-blast from the rocket launcher, it must have been fired from the ground, possibly by the corner of the hall.

"Find anything down there, Bill?"

"Not a thing."

"O.K., let's go back in."

"Hello 1, this is 11, open back door, over."

"1 Roger out."

We move back in with the OPs covering us and go through the unload procedure just inside the gate. A quick de-brief and it's up to the Mess for a brew and a think about the next patrol. The first day drawing to a close in front of the T.V. with a mug of hot, sweet tea. Mind wandering. Eyes closing, to jerk open again, guiltily. Thoughts drifting in the warmth of the tiny room...

The room is dirty, smelly, cold and damp. We look just like

the enemy we are supposed to represent. Jeans, anoraks, boots
or sneakers and the wild look that comes from being hunted.
Three days of being the I.R.A. Three days of getting into the
role of murderer. Three days of enjoying the total lawlessness
of it all.

"Listen. We'll blow up the patrol tonight. One of the
Saracens I think. A thunder flash in a bag of flour should do
the trick. Cause a bit of a stir. Where's Jones, the little shit?"
I ask, looking round at the assembled crew. There are
sniggers and sidelong looks. It takes a second or two to sink
in. "Leighton, go tell the dirty bugger that when he's finished
fucking that W.R.A.C. he'd better get his horny ass in here.
And Leighton... Come back with him." This time the place
erupts.

Outside there is the rumble of a passing armoured car.
"Get that light out. There's bound to be a patrol around."
The light goes out and we sit in the darkness; waiting;
listening. Outside there is the unmistakable tread of Army
boots. There is the rustle in the doorway and I can see in my
mind a soldier standing tucked in, rifle at the ready,
scanning the windows and the rooftops. Waiting just as we
are waiting. He moves on. Inside the house there is an
audible sigh of relief.

"Right, we'll meet up again at 2200 hrs at the junction of
Grosvenor Road and the Shankill. Bombers, you know who
you are. Jones and Leighton are the diversion, the rest of
you, as soon as the bomb goes off start something with the
troops that arrive on the scene. The object being to ensure
that the bombers escape. You know your routes you two?" A
nod of assent and then they all disperse. Some out of the back
door, some through the tunnel in the roof connecting several
houses and a couple remain here with me. Including the
W.R.A.C. Private. The waiting isn't going to be that dull
after all.

Later, and we are silent shadows creeping through the

darkened cold wet streets. Listen to every sound. Hope you've calculated the timings of the patrols correctly. A scrape of a tin can over to the left. Stop. Melt into a shadow and listen again. Round the corner at the end of the street, the sight of a rifle barrel nosing its way round the brickwork. Shit. They've slipped in an extra patrol. There's nothing to do but to carry on. Up over the wall, through the garden and lie low in a shed until the patrol passes. Think. What would I do in their position? Have a back-up, that's what. But where? All the questions bouncing through my head. Right. Leave everything, rest for ten minutes and then get on with it. Watch says ten to ten. It's going to be close.

The other three guys with me wait silently. Hope they are learning from this.

Ten minutes gone.

"Let's go. Keep down and keep quiet."

Crawl back over the wall into the street and on towards our destination. The house I'm looking for is just up the road. The roar of a Saracen in low gear gets louder. Got to get into that bloody house. It's a sprint for the last fifty metres and we make it. Just. In the door and up the stairs to be confronted with the barrel of an M1 carbine.

"Oh. It's you boss."

"Hi Jimmy. A little late I'm afraid. Ran into a patrol on the way here. I think they've been tipped off that something's in the air, so to speak."

"I think you're right. Do we go ahead?"

"Yes."

He turns to the window and waves down at the garden. The bombers are hiding behind the wall. It's like watching a movie from up here. The Saracen crawling down the street. The two bombers waiting by the wall. Waiting for the signal. Waiting...

0400 hrs. May 1976

Somewhere
Out there
Lurking
Lies our
Greatest
Fear.

"Hello 1 this is 12. Contact, wait, out."

The Ops Room goes quiet and for a long ten seconds everyone holds their breath. One of the patrols down near the border has just been zapped, but so far we don't know whether it's a bomb or gunmen. The words set the adrenalin flowing and the monster in my stomach wakes and lurches around, the wait dragging on agonisingly.

"Who is it?" The whispered question and anxious look.

"Sgt. Donne's patrol, I think."

In some of the eyes there is excitement, in me there is only dread, because tomorrow it could be me out there. The call goes through to TAC for a chopper and the stand-by section are ready and waiting by the helipad, but it is going to take time before the thing arrives. Still we wait.

Finally, Sgt. Donne calls through, his voice unsteady, shaky, panting between words. The patrol was attacked by an estimated five gunmen with automatic weapons, from a small hill close to the border. None of the patrol were hit, but one of the gunmen may have been. A loud sigh of relief goes through the Ops Room and everyone starts to breathe normally again.

The O.C. is dressed ready to go out to the scene, though why he should beats me when the whole thing is over and done with, he's just going to get in the way and be a bloody nuisance.

"Well, we can't claim a hit without a body so we will just have to wait and see if there are any funerals in Dundalk or if someone gets admitted to the hospital there. The 2I.C., tension relieved, tilts back on his chair smiling.

"Come on Clarke, you wanker, get out there."

"I'm staying right here, thank you."

"You're out that way tonight aren't you?"

"Yep, an OP in that derelict on the border for the next five days. That's why I'm not going out there now!" With that, I give him the two-fingered sign and go off to grab hold of Bill to let him know the timings for the patrol tonight. There really has been too much excitement already today.

"Quack, quack." Denny, my platoon Sgt., creeping up on my daydreaming.

"What was all the fuss about, boss?"

"Eddie just got jumped on the border by some gunmen. No casualties, but he didn't sound too happy."

"Oh well, such is life. When are you out tonight?"

"A Puma's coming in at 2200 hrs to pick us up. We get dropped off about two thousand metres away and march in to the OP site."

"You seen the weather forecast? I doubt you'll be getting a helicopter tonight. Rain. Quack, quack."

"Oh cheers, aren't you the optimist. Just what I need, to struggle across country in the rain at night. Fuck this cunting place."

"Now, now, boss." He goes off making Donald Duck noises.

I find Bill and give him the timings for briefings and disappear off to the cookhouse to make sure all the rations are ready.

"The choppers can't fly because of the weather, Tony." The O.C. telling me what I've already guessed. "But TAC have offered us a Q van."

"No way!" says I emphatically. "No way. The local Provo unit in Newry sent TAC a list of all the Q cars and vans with registration numbers, makes and colours. Don't tell me TAC have changed the colours. No. I'd rather walk, even on a night like tonight."

"Well, it's there if you want it. The S.A.S. use them."

"Maybe, but not in this area. Christ, if the other side got wind of one moving around here, you'd never find the bits!"

"When do you plan on leaving, then?"

"In an hour."

Drive around this area in a Q van? Some of these guys live in cloud-cuckoo land. The only reason we stay alive down here is by not giving the I.R.A. the opportunity to hit us. Q vans indeed!

The lads are sitting in the briefing-room, yawning, cam-cream-covered faces looking odd in the clean white room. I tell them that all the forced marches we did in Aldershot are going to pay off because there ain't no helicopters. Chorus of cheers and swearing.

Route explained, we are by the gate and as each man steps out into the night, there is the metallic clicking of rifles being cocked. It's five thousand metres as the crow flies to our destination, but on foot in the pouring rain across country it is going to take us all night just to get halfway. It is blacker than hell with the rain driving into our faces, soaking through our smocks and freezing us before we've gone a couple of hundred yards. The only thing making us do this is discipline and lack of imagination. I try to think of nothing but the job in hand, otherwise I would start jumping at my own shadow and not get ten feet before becoming a nervous wreck. The howling wind and the rain all join together to make the whole thing freaky as hell.

The route takes us well clear of the houses, round the outskirts of the town, at first moving west, then south, and finally turning east to circle round the little cluster of houses called Monog. A large hill rises up behind the village like a brooding black dinosaur, trees like spikes flailing around in the wind. The grass in the fields is tall and thick and wet, making walking difficult and filling our boots with water. At least walking uphill like this the exertion keeps us warm, but at every hedge we have to stop, collect together, go through, stop again, collect again and when the last man is through move off once more. It is time-consuming and energy sapping but essential. Bombs and booby traps don't go to sleep at night.

At last, after what seems an age, we are on top of the hill. We quickly move away from the skyline into the lee of the hill and settle down for a brief rest and sort out the rest of the route. I'm doing the map-reading and leading, which is really by feel and instinct as the features are not recognisable in this weather, so taking bearings on an object is a waste of time.

"We are never going to get in tonight, boss."

"You're right Bill, but we've got to get as close as possible so that tomorrow night we can take our time moving in. Where's Cpl. Jonson?"

"Just following up my tail end."

"O.K. boss, all in now." Cpl. Jonson appearing out of the darkness, rain dripping down his beret on to his face and off his nose.

"We'll make a firm base about here," I say, pointing to the map which is lit by a pinpoint of light from a torch cupped in my hand, "and hole up until midnight tomorrow. It is going to take us until first light to get there at the rate we have been going, so for Christ's sake don't let anybody lag behind."

"O.K. boss."

"Let's go."

I haul my sodden body off the ground, rearrange the pack on my aching shoulders, snuggle my S.L.R. into the crook of my arm and we are off again. It is not so much the contacts with gunmen that scare the hell out of me, it's walking into a booby trap or stepping on a landmine. In the dark like this there is no way of being able to scan the ground for likely areas, you just put one foot in front of the other and hope. I don't find it exciting in the least. It scares the living shit out of me.

The rain stopped an hour ago with the beginnings of dawn. That time of the day that gently pushes aside the night, the mist hanging in the valleys like cobwebs, draped over the trees, wrapped around the edges of hills, hiding small farms that gradually poke their chimneys through the greyness as the mist disperses with a slight stirring of a breeze. I look at the lads spread around the hollow of rock we found, pale faces smudged with cam-cream that has all but come off with the rain and the exertion. Some are falling asleep in their soggy clothes, others are making a brew.

"I've put the three guns up on the edges of the hollow, boss, with good views and fields of fire. You've just got to work out the stags for your patrol."

"Cheers, Bill." Turning to my radio op. "Smith, have you got a brew on yet?"

"Just coming boss."

All the talk is in whispers, all the movements slow and deliberate. Undoing the pack of rations takes time if we're not to make any noise. The whole thing now being second nature. Rubbish is carried with us until we get back to base, dirty tins sitting in a pack for five days gradually growing mould. Smith brings a steaming mug of tea and we sit sharing it in the gathering light, him sitting there with his headphones on listening to the radio traffic, me hunched over the map going through the route tonight and all the possibilities about being compromised. The particular derelict we are going to is literally right on the border and has been the scene of OPs before, which were discontinued after a particularly nasty incident when it was attacked with mortar and small-arms fire. Anyway, I figured it might be worth the risk of putting one in, to monitor the traffic across the border. The success of the thing depends on whether we can get in unseen and remain that way until we finish. If we get spotted there are going to be a lot of nervous soldiers about. Shit, what did I volunteer for? I've got to have a loose cog in my brain.

"Did you see London's rifle sir, where the bullet smashed it? He was a lucky fucker, he said the rounds went between his legs. Shit, he was a lucky fucker." Smith talking to himself more than me.

"They reckon they got one of the cunts though. Saw him being dragged off by one of the others."

I grunt an acknowledgement. I wonder what's going through his mind? What went through mine when I was that age? Envy? Thinking to himself and wondering what it must be like to come under fire like that?

Don't think. I've been there and it is a scary thing. Something you can best do without, I want this to be a nice peaceful tour. What am I saying, we hadn't been here two minutes and a chopper was hit, then some idiot of an S.A.S. officer shot some guy he said was trying to take his rifle off him and caused a storm because nobody believed a word of it. Then a whole carload of S.A.S. got picked up in the Republic in a civilian car in civilian clothes and armed to the teeth. The excuse was that they got lost. Well, if that's the élite then what the fuck must the rest of us be like? Cowboys, the lot of them; there are some guys I've recognised who have failed our selection tests, so how did they get into the S.A.S? I wouldn't give them the time of day. A few years ago after the Belfast tour, we took part in an exercise as enemy, with them. After a couple of days we were asked to take twenty-four hours off to give them a chance to regroup because we had completely compromised all their R.V. points. They are a joke.

Still, it's not worth getting hot under the collar, it just annoys me when guys like us, who spend all the time on the ground doing the donkey-work, get the worst equipment and the cannon-fodder tasks. Shit, this whole mess is getting to me.

Luckily the sun came out during the day and we were able to get our clothes dry. Nobody has been near us all day, so hopefully they don't know we are in the area. With the return of another night, the clouds start forming overhead and pretty soon we are going to be in for another rainstorm. Quack, quack. Just what we need to start five days without being able to move or talk or anything.

The patrol into the OP site has gone well so far, with nobody sighted and the village, just before the border, passed without so much as a dog barking. The lads are working well and I'm glad we managed to get a rest after last night's trek through the rain; it has made all the difference. The closer we get the more alert we get, stopping at the slightest sound, listening for long minutes, eyes trying to pierce the darkness and interpret the shapes. Buildings take on a sinister presence; trees become giants hovering over us, waiting to strike. Every stonewall, every gatepost, every hedge hides a bomb and as the imagination starts to take over, I stop to take control of myself again and be rational. Exercises were never like this.

The other members of the patrol seem to be totally unconcerned as we near our objective. Cpl. Menzies and Cpl. Jonson break off and take their patrols to their positions. I have organised it so that my patrol mans the actual OP site and the others cover our rear and over to the hill where previously the mortar attack had been launched from. I've chosen a spot just away from the derelict, not trusting the place for fear of booby traps; in the junction of two walls, which will give us cover from fire as well as view. It is full of six-foot-high stinging nettles, so requires some careful work to get right into the middle of it.

There is a large tree overhanging the wall so we can stand watching the road quite happily without being seen. I've brought along a small tape-recorder so that we don't have to write anything down, just whisper all the information.

"Smith, signal 1 in position," I whisper in the radio op's ear, and the OP is operational. Home for the next four days. Two on stag at a time, one at the observation point, the other guarding. The two not on stag sleep. Four hours on, four hours off, staggered so that while one is starting, the other is into his last two hours. Watch, guard, eat out of tins, no cooking allowed, sleep and then begin the whole process again. The longer you remain in these things, the greater the risk of being compromised. Four young soldiers were killed in a border OP when they fell asleep in their sleeping bags and were shot whilst trying to escape. The lesson was painfully simple. Drop your guard just once and the bastards will get you. All these thoughts going through my head as I take my stag and whisper the registration numbers of passing cars into the tape and watch as a farmer cycles past whistling to himself in the rain.

The hours drag on and eventually the rota becomes the only way of knowing which day it is. Day succeeds night succeeds day in a monotonous cycle enriched with the cold wind and the rain; the unceasing rain. Smith snores when he sleeps and so has to be shaken awake whenever he makes a noise. The others are getting restless after the long period of inactivity; the strict self-discipline that OP routine imposes begins to gnaw away at the senses, feed the imagination, and sap the energy with the constant tension and knowledge that we are alone out here, with our skill and our instincts to keep us alive.

To pass the time whilst on the observation point, the Toms have been passing messages to each other over the tape, telling jokes and swearing at each other, describing each other asleep. All in whispers. As I listen, it is all I can do to stop from bursting into loud laughter. Sanity is a tape-machine and a ceaseless store of jokes. Sanity is kidding yourself that you are far better than the opposition.

Sitting here in the silence of the Irish night, listening to the gentle patter of the rain falling down through the tree branches to drip with consistent accuracy onto my hand clutching my rifle. Looking at the ghostly green countryside through the image-intensifying sight gives me the feeling of unreality and light-headedness that is usually associated with good Moroccan cannabis. I'm high as a kite on tension and exhaustion, a very dangerous condition to be in, but it is so nice! Just twenty-four hours to go before I lift the OP and we head off to the L.Z. for an early morning pick-up.

Lifting an OP is always a dodgy procedure, when the senses are at their lowest after days of little sleep, with the cold and the wet eating into your energy reserves. We are out without incident, and heading toward the L.Z. for a pick-up at 0430 hrs, just as the dawn begins to break. It doesn't take long to get there and after posting the sentries with the guns, we can relax a little and let the lads brew up the first hot drink in four days.

"Did you see anything, boss?"

"Not a thing. Still we have to check out the cars that we logged, though I doubt that they will produce anything. It was worth a try." I try to sound convincing, but know that we have really just wasted the time and put ourselves at risk for nothing.

"When are we out next?"

"Tomorrow." Bill groans and shakes his tired head.

"Not another OP I trust. I couldn't fucking stand that."

"No, just a three-day area foot patrol." Twenty-four hours to rest up, get all the equipment sorted, clothes washed, write a letter home and then out again. That means we get the chance of a couple of good meals before we're back on the gut-wrenching compo.

"Chopper in two minutes, sir."

"O.K. Smith. Right, get your kit together lads."

The muted sound of rotor blades becomes a roar as the Puma sweeps low overhead, goes into a tight banked turn and drops down onto the L.Z. in a beautifully executed flare. As the wheels touch down, the lads are off and running to scramble aboard. Time on the ground no more than thirty seconds, before we are off and flying low over the hedgerows and fields. This is the part I enjoy most, feeling the exhilaration of low-flying helicopter flights, the gut-lurching turns and drops, the countryside spread below and the pleasure of not having to walk back with aching shoulders and sore feet.

In no time at all we are passing over Crossmaglen, lying in its hollow like any other sleepy country village; the base looking like an obscene sculpture on the green landscape.

Round the football field and we are flaring in to land on the helipad, feeling like the returning survivors of the Legion of the Damned. The back gate is open and we go through to unload, taking the round out of the chamber and replacing it in the magazine.

"Clean weapons before you do anything else. Section commanders to carry out an inspection," I yell above the rising clamour of the Puma taking off. "After that, a quick de-brief then eat and sleep."

They shuffle off to the billets looking like little old men, now that the tension has gone and the tiredness creeps up on them. I follow, mind in neutral, to file my patrol report and drop the tapes into the Int. cell for them to sort out.

"Hello you wanker," comes the cheerful voice of the 2I.C., but I'm not in the mood.

"Fuck off," says I.

"You can't crack me," he laughs.

"Quack, fucking quack," is my only comment before going up to my bunk to clean my weapon and sort out my kit.

There is a guy looking at me from the mirror. Hollow, red-rimmed eyes with a lost expression, set in a stubble-covered, brown, streaked, wind-blown face, topped by dirty matted hair. I've seen him before on numerous occasions but after a shower, shave, eat and sleep he disappears to be replaced by a pallid spectre, thin and emaciated.

It is difficult to realise that it is still only 0530 early morning. So the only meal available at this time is a plateful of greasy eggs and bacon with chips and bread, washed down by the everlasting cup of tea. After five days of cold food out of tins, this is heaven and it is hard not to bolt the food down as quickly as possible. The lads are sitting quietly, eating away with little or nothing to say to each other, some nodding off to sleep over their black plastic mugs, others going through the motions of small talk to a non-existent audience. What is there to discuss at 0530 in the morning when you're exhausted? Sleep, give me sleep.

It seems only minutes ago since my head hit the pillow and I zonked straight out, but my watch tells me it has been eight hours. I fall back onto the pillow and look at the darkened room, with thin slivers of light coming through the gaps between the sandbags and the breeze blocks. It is taller than it's wide or deep, and my smock hanging on a nail on the door brushes my face if I turn over that way. The door doesn't fully open because the bed is in the way and in my drowsy state I'm trying to figure out how they got the bed into the room in the first place.

Asleep, and this is a cosy little den, away from all the danger and hassle. Awake it becomes a claustrophobic cupboard, pressing in and suffocating. So once fully awake, I get out of bed, dress and make my way into the Mess to see what is going on.

Pat, one of the platoon commanders, is there shovelling food into his mouth as fast as his hand can move. The N.C.O.s have several names for him, the politest being "Doom" and "J.C.B." The first refers to his non-existent qualities as a soldier, and the second to the way he eats his food. He looks up with food spilling out of his mouth and I think that I can do without this, having just woken up.

"Finally got out of bed, mattress-back," he says to me, spitting some food onto the table.

"Don't push your luck, son," says I, to put him back in his place. Jesus, I can't stand the little prick.

He goes a bit pink and carries on eating. I turn and notice the C.S.M. behind me curled up with silent laughter. He can't stand the shit either.

"Afternoon Sar'nt Major."

"Hello sir," he says, barely able to keep a straight face. The longer young Pat stays out of our sight the better we like it.

"Cup of tea, Sar'nt Major?" I ask and pour out a cup to his nod.

"You're going to have to go steady on the twenty-four-hour packs sir, because it looks like we are going to have to use them."

"Why, for fuck's sake?"

"It seems there is a shortage of meat rations and the next resup isn't due for another week."

"Oh great. Fucking-A. That is really going to boost morale."

"Sorry sir, but there is little we can do about it."

Now what the hell are we going to do? Out for three days with little or no food. We can't stop patrolling just because there is no food, so it is one pack for two men for twenty-four hours. Just have to supplement it with goodie bars from the Paki in the canteen. How did I ever get into this in the first place?

"O.K. Sar'nt Major, we'll sort something out." You can't crack me, I'm a rubber duck.

Oh well, down to the Ops Room and find out what has been happening whilst I've been kipping.

"Ah Tony, just the man," the O.C. says, leaping up the stairs.

"I've got an alteration to your patrol for tomorrow. Instead of going up to Cullyhanna, I want you to concentrate on the area directly south, down near the border. It hasn't been covered so far and I want a good patrol there." I follow him into his room and we discuss the changes over the map of the area.

"Okey-dokey. Will do Major. Presumably we are out at the same time?"

"Yes, no change on that. The drop-off point will be the same as well, so that you can come back in through Monog and clear that area of the town." That over, I carry on with what I started and go on down to the Ops Room. The 2I.C. is still there.

"Has the O.C. seen you?"

"Yes, just now."

"At least I persuaded him to leave the rest of the programme alone. He wanted to change it all around." He doesn't sound too happy.

"Now, now, no cracking please," I say, just to goad him a bit.

"Sometimes the man is a fucking idiot. If I didn't walk out occasionally I'd hit him." He fumes on a bit longer, asking me, as I get on with the O.C. or rather the O.C. gets on with me, whether I could have a word with him about some of the patrols. There's no point though. As he said, the man's an idiot. Nice, but an idiot just the same.

"Will you take over while I get some scoff in me?" he says.

"Go on then, just don't be too long. I've got things to do, you know."

"I'll be as long as I like," he says, flexing his rank. Sometimes he gets a little short-tempered, our 2I.C. The other week he had a full-scale row with one of the pub owners in the town, in the end almost threatening to kill the bloke. On reflection perhaps we should have let him do it, instead of dragging him out. It would have been one less of the bastards. After showing me who was out on the ground and where they were, he goes off and leaves me with the crackle of the radio, the radio op, and a pack of playing cards. So I settle down to a game of patience and wait, listening to the sounds of the camp.

Crossmaglen.

Cross to the locals. X.M.G. to us. A piece of news, soon to be forgotten, to the rest of the world. I think back to a conversation that occurred in the Mess in Aldershot one night, with an officer spouting about how the risks were very small in Ulster. Then I look at the anti-mortar wire, the gun positions, the sandbags, intruder alarm systems and everything else and begin to wonder where that guy is at. Perhaps all these things are just bluff. Perhaps he knows something the rest of us have yet to learn.

It is in moments like these that I wish I was back safely at home, away from it all. Not just an idle wish, but a fervent longing.

The border stretches away on either side as we lie on the hill scanning the green fields and hillocks with the binoculars. The border, with a thousand crossing points and myriads of wires leading from firing points in the Republic to landmines on the roads and in the hedges of Ulster. Beyond the hedge in front is a sanctuary for the terrorists. A place that, under international law, we are not allowed to fire our weapons into. We are not going to observe that, of course. Who in their right mind would sit and get shot at without returning fire?

"Bill, we are going to head towards the border crossing at Drumackavall and head up towards this road junction here." I point to it on the map, and gesture in the direction.

"We'll patrol as we have been, but when we get to the junction I want you up on this hillock to cover the rear and Cpl. Edge on the other side on this feature, covering over towards Drumackavall itself."

"O.K. boss." Cpl. Edge nods his assent and we prepare to move.

For once it is not raining, which really makes a change, and the lads, although tired, are working well and patrolling with care. There is no need to check that they are going to the right positions when we stop, it has become second nature.

As we go, I check the locations on the map of previous bomb incidents and make sure we skirt the actual detonation sites. The I.R.A. have never heard of the phrase "lightning never strikes twice in the same place" and have a nasty habit of putting bombs back in the craters of the last ones. Over the past few weeks, we have found two firing points, by lying on top of the wires where they come out of the ground. Instead of clearing them we are going to leave them for a possible lure operation at a later date.

"Hello 11, this is 1, send location over."

"11 wait out."

Working down close to the border not far from Crossmaglen, I carry a small Pye Pocketphone radio as well as having the large backpacked A41. It makes life easier for controlling the sections and sending P. Checks and car checks. We stop and I quickly work out the location in code and send it back.

They don't say anything, just carry on with the butts of the rifles pulled more firmly into the shoulders, and heads swivelling from side to side with extra concentration.

Outwardly I'm calm and unconcerned, as I casually negotiate a ditch and scramble up the other side. Inside I'm coming apart at the seams, fighting the rising fear and the temptation to find a hole and crawl into it. The wind teasingly brushes my face and moans mockingly through the trees and bushes, taunting me with its gentle sighs in the waving grass. Somehow we make it to the road with no incident and the two other patrols take up their cover positions, before I move on down to set the V.C.P. I hope the cover groups are in the right places. There is nothing to do but act casual. This may be the only opportunity to get one of the buggers, if we can just give the impression that everything is fine and dandy. Jesus, I hope those cover groups are in the right places.

Just to lend a bit of authenticity to my play-acting, I stroll slowly across the road, in full view of any potential sniper positions. This is where I find out whether the other patrol commanders are thinking what I'm thinking.

I turn to look down the road to the border and glance up at the menacing Drumackavall feature, scene of so many deaths. That's where I expect any shots to come from.

The low, loud crack of an S.L.R. knifes through the stillness and my already tense muscles leap into action and spring me across the road to the cover of a stone wall.

"Come on lads, get your fucking arses over here."

They follow and thud down onto the earth, breathing shallowly and quickly. Thinking to myself, I realise that it was an S.L.R. and therefore one of ours, so the cover group must have spotted something.

All this before the sound of the second shot dies away. The strike is plainly visible from the still-lingering dust kicked up by the rounds hitting the rocks about 100 metres up the hill from us.

No time to think, just yell for the cover group to stay there and then start skirmishing up the hill. As I run, I can see Cpl. Menzies and his patrol flying over the ground to my right.

"Hello 1 this is 11, contact wait out." Panted out whilst still running up the hill. No time to worry about bombs or bullets, just get up the hill and fall apart later.

I'm aware that the firing has ceased and that the only sound is the thud of boots and the rasping pants from scared and tired Toms. At the top, there is nothing. Only the chipped rock and long scores in the ground from the strikes. It is then that I become aware of a different sound, the familiar clattering of a helicopter. The voice of the pilot comes over the static and asks if I want any help. There is no point, as whoever was up here has gone. Cpl. Menzies joins me having made a quick recce of the immediate area.

"Nothing boss. Shall I take my patrol over to the Drumackavall and have a look around there?"

"No. We'll all go together. Wait until Cpl. Edge gets here and he can cover us across."

In a few minutes, having given my report and intentions to Company H.Q., we are on our way again. This time out to get someone, and whoever or whatever moves is going to get a 7.62 straight between the eyes.

Over on the other side of the feature, a tractor is moving across the field, seemingly totally unaware of what has been happening. As we move across towards him, Cpl. Edge comes up on the radio.

"Hello 11, this is 11B, we've found something here, request your company, over."

"11 Roger out."

"Bill, grab that guy on the tractor and bring him over here."

As Cpl. Menzies gets the guy off the tractor, I make my way back to where Cpl. Edge is standing peering at something in the grass.

"We haven't touched anything, boss. It's just as we found it." Lying in the grass is an Armalite 30-round magazine with rounds in it, and close by a clip of what look to be armour-piercing Garrand rounds. Well, well, what fun.

"Bill get that bloke over here. O.K. lads, get over there by the hedge and get down."

This is a precaution because the I.R.A. have a nasty habit of scattering rounds about in apparent disorder, one of which is attached to a piece of thread which in its turn is connected to a pull-switch detonator of a large bomb. Lift the round and little pieces of you are spread all over the fields. Now is the time to find out if this is one of those.

"Well, what do you know about these, Paddy?"

"Nothin'. Nothin' at all. This isn't even my land." He looks pale and very nervous.

"I see. Then how would you like to pick them up for me?"

"N-n-no," he stammers, now looking visibly scared.

"Right, take this guy over there and keep the gun on him. If I go up, shoot the bastard. So Paddy, for your sake and mine, I hope there is nothing on the end of these."

He's shaking now and I feel just the same way. Mouth like parchment and knees that want to rattle uncontrollably. What the hell am I doing this for? Why don't I get one of the Toms to do it? The answer is simple, if one of the Toms did it and it blew, I would never be able to live with myself. Deep breath. Bend down, fingers shaking.

"Remember, if I go, he goes."

The only thing to do is to snatch it quickly. My fingers close around the cold metal of the magazine and jerk it off the ground. Nothing. The birds are still singing in the trees and there's a look of disappointment on a couple of the Toms' faces who would dearly love to blast Paddy. One down, one to go.

The clip of Garrand rounds comes off the ground just as neatly and I heave an inward sigh of relief, straighten up and look hard as nails.

"Bring the cunt over here."

Paddy looks ashen-faced and I'm thinking that he thought there just may have been something under there. We P. Check him, tell Company H.Q. of the find and wait for the O.C. to get his brain working and sort something out. For the moment, it's sit down and let some of the tension dissipate with the lengthening shadows of the afternoon sun.

1200 hrs. June 1976

It seems to me
That beauty
Hides an
Ugly
Soul.

The television newsreaders have been informing us that the weather in England is hot and dry. They should be so lucky. The fields here are growing greener with the rain that falls most days. A little sun would be a pleasant thing.

There are pictures of rubber ducks all over my platoon Sgt's shed and a Tom in another platoon has been making a collection of pub signs and garden gnomes and has them adorning the entrance to his bunk. The craziness helps restore the balance after the seriousness of the patrols, OPs and other duties.

My platoon has just started a week on base duties and town patrols, which means I have to spend most of my time, when not on patrol, manning the Ops Desk. The never-ending game of patience is spread on the desk and as usual I'm losing.

"Chopper in two minutes, sir," the radio op wakes me from my reverie on the weather.

"Is this the one with Sgt. Donne's patrol on?" he says.

"Yep," says I.

They are returning from hospital after a check-up. Two days ago, they were blown up on a hill near the border. One of the Toms, Pte. Snowdon, was critically injured and the others miraculously suffered only fairly minor wounds. The bomb was detonated by a radio-controlled device from the other side of the border, and it was buried in the bottom of a hedgerow. Part of it failed to explode which was lucky for the rest of the patrol, otherwise most of them would now be dead. There is a feeling of impotence in the base at the inability to react. We just sit here like stuffed dummies and pretend it didn't happen. The order has come down that we must not let the locals know just how bad Pte. Snowdon is; even if he dies we have to pretend he is alive and getting better. What a farce! The truth is he died.

The noise of the helicopter reduces as it lands, then rises as it takes off again to fly back to the comparative safety of Bessbrook. By switching on the intercom I can hear the tinny greeting of the guard by the back gate and the sound of weapons being unloaded. The everyday sounds of an Army on peacekeeping duties in South Armagh, as homely as the clink of milk bottles or letterbox flap in the morning, back in England.

"Helipad, tell Sgt. Donne that the O.C. wants to see him."

"Yes sir."

Somehow, I get the feeling that the O.C. doesn't like Sgt. Donne and I know for certain that it is reciprocated. In fact, there has even been the odd comment about rolling a grenade into his bunk. All one big happy family!

One of the Toms brings in the latest consignment of feature films and the all-important mail.

In Belfast, I used to hate the hours spent on the Ops Desk, now they form the nucleus of a safe place to stay. The longer I'm here, the less time I have to spend on the ground. To sit and while away the hours reading, daydreaming, playing patience, provides the anaesthetic required to forget the nerve-racking OPs and lure patrols.

Last week we did a lure on one of the bombs we found near the border on a road. Young Pat was supposed to place the ambush on the firing point and I had to put a V.C.P. on the bomb as a lure in the hope that someone would try and have a go at us. It's just as well nobody tried, as I found out, by tripping over him, that the stupid incompetent had put the ambush in the wrong place with no chance of hitting the bombers if they had been there. It was all I could do not to shoot the bastard on the spot. The nickname the Toms had given him was sure accurate. Why more people don't get killed with idiots like him in the Army, I don't know! It took three days before I could sleep again, as I kept waking, thinking of standing on top of five hundred pounds of explosive. There's no way I'm doing any more operations with him, that's for sure.

Got to stop thinking of things like this and put the mind back into neutral, stare at the map, not seeing. Think of the odd things that you can see in this place, like taking a step back in time. Like the last country patrol when we were checking farmhouses hidden away in neglected corners, in lonely backwaters of civilisation. On a couple of occasions we came across farms that I was going to list as derelict when there was movement inside. At first, we were about to dive for cover when our fear turned to sheer amazement as a couple appeared at the door. To say they lived in squalor would be understating it. Dirt was ingrained into their skin and fleas hopped around their clothes. Their teeth had completely disintegrated and their hair was matted into filthy knots. It was like something out of *Quatermass and the Pit*. There was no water or electricity in the house at all and the bedding consisted of old newspapers and other sundry items such as old animal feed sacks.

Now sitting here, I'm not sure that it existed. Maybe I just hallucinated. I may have done, but not the rest of the patrol I had with me. The other farm was almost as bad and had an old hermit living there.

South Armagh, still light-years away from civilisation, still living in the dark ages, where barbarity and cruelty are the prime factors of a successful life. Where stealing and killing are as natural a part of living as breathing is to most of us.

Having been relieved for lunch and enjoyed a short break I'm back behind the desk, sipping the strong tea out of my huge china mug. It has been too quiet over the past few days, with nothing happening and even the locals being fairly tolerant. Very unusual! Sgt. Donne sticks his head round the door:

"Was it a frog
That sat on a log
On the Monog.

Or was it a toad

That crossed the road."

He recites, and then vanishes to the cries of "Rivet, rivet." Obviously the O.C. is riding high in the popularity stakes at the moment. Light relief in the oppressive atmosphere.

The Ops Desk may provide the safety of sandbagged walls, and the illusion of impregnability but it leaves the mind open to wander through the paths of memory and dwell upon the waste and sadness generated by Ulster.

Not long ago, I had taken my patrol up to the ranges at Ballykinler to zero our weapons and what started as a relaxing day turned into one of sourness and sadness. On the way back, with the weather, as usual, wet and windy, we were involved in an accident with a Saracen just returning to Ballykinler from Bessbrook. The driver of the Saracen was clearly going too fast and when he tried to take action to avoid our three-ton trucks, he slid, hit the bank and turned over. There was a young soldier standing in the turret who was crushed as the vehicle went over. Although he was alive for a short time, all our efforts failed and he died on a lonely stretch of Irish road, in the rain.

I can clearly see his expression as the life went out of him and his eyes glazed and I can remember the feeling welling inside me as I thought of the waste and the stupidity. As if there were not enough danger, this young lad with four days left of his two-year tour was dead and I was starting to blame him now for the resurgence of my revulsion for this whole thing.

"Hello boss, book us out will you. Town patrol."

The voice of my platoon Sgt. shakes me away from those dangerous thoughts and back to the job.

"Will do. Which route are you taking?"

"Through the Rathview estate, back through the town and then I thought I may take a look at the church. Then back in round the outskirts of the town."

"Fine, keep your head down."

"Of course, don't I always," he says and walks out quacking away.

Well, the good old rain has started again and by the sound of it, some thunder and lightning on the way too. I'm tired after a long day sitting listening to the radio and playing patience and am looking forward to a good sleep before my duty starts again in five hours time. Sitting on the edge of my bed in tee shirt and denims and boots, thinking of the list of things I must check before I go to sleep. Suddenly there is the loud hammering of the G.P.M.G. up in one of the OPs. Here we go again. Grab rifle and race downstairs to the Ops Room where there is pandemonium.

"There are some gunmen over by the estate," comes the cry over the intercom from the OP, above the noise of the machine gun.

The Sergeant Major is there, half-dressed as I am, and some of the stand-by section.

"I'll take these out through the back gate and over to the hall," I tell the duty Ops officer and race out to the back gate. It is pouring with rain, as if the heavens suddenly opened and deposited the lot over this small piece of Ulster. The lightning splits the dark and outlines the entire landscape in a brief second before the thunder crashes again, wiping it out in an instant, plunging us back into complete blackness.

"Hey, in the OP."

"Yeah."

"We're going out to the hall. Keep an eye on us through the I.W.S."

"Will do."

With the gun now silent, the only sounds are the crashing of thunder and the splattering of rain on the tin roofs and the mud now collecting in the compound. Rifles at the ready, peering into the black night, crouching at each flash of lightning and trying to imprint the scene on our memories before we fumble forward a few paces.

The Sgt. Major is right behind me, and in the brief, brilliant flashes when I turn around, I can see the rain pouring over his head, plastering his hair down and sticking his vest to his body. There is nothing by the hall, so I lead the way towards the estate, falling over invisible objects, staggering into low walls and finally making it to the spot where the gun rounds had taken great chunks out of the brickwork. Nothing. If there had been anybody they would have been long gone anyway, but it was worth checking it out. Sometimes people in a hurry drop things; not this time.

The procession back to the rear gate of the base is a comedy of falling over, bumping into each other and swearing. We get back in and I tell the OP to keep his eyes open and only to fire if he sees anything and can be certain of hitting it.

Back to the Ops Room and report.

"You stupid idiots, what do you mean by going out without a radio. We couldn't contact you, had no way of knowing what was going on. You ever do that again and I'm going to charge you."

The O.C. greets us with a mouthful and I'm standing here soaking wet with the tension still on me getting a little angry.

"The OP had us in view all the time and if you wanted to know what was happening you only had to ask him."

"Don't talk to me that way."

I can see this is going to get a bit silly and the Sgt. Major has already walked out in disgust.

"If we had waited to get kitted out with radio and all the works, then if there had been somebody still out there, he would have left out of boredom from waiting. You know as well as I do that the only way to get these guys is to react quickly, otherwise they're gone."

"That's not the point. SOPs state that you must have a radio and flak jacket when on patrol in the town."

Oh Jesus! I'm getting even more angry now and if the 2I.C. hadn't stepped in, I would have done something violent. SOPs for God's sake. Where does he think he is? Back in Aldershot writing out the orders for the guard? The 2I.C. tactfully ushers me away and I go on up to my bunk. The Sgt. Major is in the Mess pouring out a couple of large mugs of tea.

"Here you are sir."

"Cheers," I say and slump down into one of the chairs, rainwater still dripping off my head and squelching around in my boots.

"Take no notice, sir, you know he's an idiot. He hasn't a fucking clue how to run a Company."

Well loyalty can only go so far and mine is running a bit thin after that exchange downstairs, so I just nod in agreement.

"The lads are getting pissed off with him too," the Sgt. Major says, sipping the scalding liquid.

"Yes I know, that's why I go on these long patrols. At least out there we are on our own and can just concentrate on the job. What the fuck's the use of trying to argue with him, he's got blinkers on."

We sit there, soaking wet, drinking our tea and ruminating on the immediate events.

Above the sound of the thunder, comes the unmistakable boom of a large bomb exploding away to the south. The ground shakes momentarily and the Sgt. Major and I look at each other.

"We haven't got anyone to the south sir," he says to my questioning look and I relax again and get on with drinking my tea.

"If he wants me to go down and check that out, he's got another thing coming. Not tonight. No way," I say and the Sgt. Major laughs.

"It's probably the lightning set it off anyway. Still, that's one less of the fuckers."

Christ, what a night! All I want to do is get a little sleep.

"Well, I'm off to bed, I can't stand the pace any longer," I say, and take the five steps to my cupboard.

The O.C. has decided to put a twenty-four-hour watch on the farm close to where we found the magazine and rounds, which is O.K., except he wants me to do it and he wants to come. Just what I need at the moment. I have been getting the increasing feeling that the I.R.A. are going to set a booby trap around the base somewhere, as opposed to a straight shoot-out; so that makes life just a little more risky and even more so if we have to look out for the O.C. at the same time.

So here we are struggling through hedges again at the dead of night, cursing inwardly at the torn denims and flesh, sweating with the exertion, trying to get to the farm as quickly as possible in order to get the maximum time on surveillance.

The O.C. is behind me and I know he hasn't a clue where we are, just following on like the rest of the Toms. Out here, I'm the boss. This is my element and I'm good at this sort of thing. The radio crackles.

"Hello 11, this is 1, send location over." The voice of the 2I.C. carries to those with radios.

"11 wait out," I whisper, call a halt, explain quickly what I am doing, work out the code and send it back.

"1 Roger out," comes the reply, followed by "Rivet, rivet. Quack, quack." Smith, who had the backpacked set turned on, sniggers and I hear a whispering going back through the patrol accompanied by giggles.

The O.C. seems oblivious to it all as he hunches down over a map trying to figure out where we are. The patrol continues and just down in the valley ahead lies our objective, snuggling amongst the trees, innocently asleep in the moonlight. Beyond it rears the menacing Drumackavall feature, black against the night sky.

The house itself is as quiet as the grave of a hundred soldiers and we circle it looking into the outhouses and taking the registration numbers of the cars sitting in the forecourt. They clear out on the computer, unfortunately, so we have no excuse to enter the house, just retire to a safe distance and watch.

The cover groups are in position, and the O.C. is with me in my surveillance group in the bottom of a hedgerow. It's a bit like playing hide and seek. This game, however, goes on for far too long, trying to stay awake in the hours before dawn when not even a wild animal is creeping about. It all seems so pointless. Grown-ups playing children's games with death the only winner. The O.C. is lying just five metres away from me and every now and then, the bulbous eyes close and his head drops slowly onto the ground, to jerk up again with a look of annoyance. On the other side of me, Smith starts to grunt every now and again as he drops off in a doze and I have to kick him awake. To try and pass the time, I look at the moon and the stars moving in the heavens watching over our puerile game. All the wisdom of the centuries locked up in the never-changing movements of the planets and constellations and in the memory of non-existent exploding stars, shining in the sky.

As the dawn draws nearer, so it gets colder, the dew penetrating our bones and stiffening them, making it more uncomfortable by the minute. The lifting shadows and arriving grey pre-dawn take the decision and after a night of discomfort and inaction we are off, back to base moving slowly and confidently in the early-morning stillness.

An explosion shatters the morning air and echoes through the trees, the ground rumbling under our feet. It's come from the direction of the base.

"Follow me, I want a V.C.P. on the Dundalk road. Cpl. Edge to the north and Cpl. Menzies to the south. Come on you cunts, move yourselves."

O.C. hasn't moved and is standing frozen like the first time this happened to us. Once the rumble of the explosion has died away, the silence reasserts itself and the birds continue to sing in the bushes and trees. After what seems an age we arrive panting at the Dundalk road once again and set the V.C.P.

The O.C. has collared Smith and is trying to find out what has happened. The only answer we get is that my platoon Sgt. found a booby trap and there is one slight casualty. There is a sinking feeling inside me as my overactive imagination gets to work and it takes a superhuman effort to stop from cracking here and now. Just get on with the job, it's what you're paid for! No cars on the road at this time and for sure nobody is going to venture out immediately after an incident. So after a few minutes we start patrolling back towards the base, this time ignoring all the safety precautions and moving on the road.

Turn left at the hall and move in through the rear gate. The O.C. goes hurriedly through to the Ops Room whilst I check that the weapons are cleared. I can hear him ranting through the walls as I make my way to the main building.

"You fool, I've a good mind to have you busted for this. Can't you do a thing that you're told, you people? If I say don't touch anything, that's precisely what I mean."

Sgt. Denny is sitting in the Ops Room, pale and dazed with his legs burnt, denims in tatters and boots ripped to shreds. He is in shock and the words are not penetrating. The O.C. rants on a bit longer and then storms out, not even bothering to ask how Sgt. Denny is.

"Hey Jimmy, can you hear me?" I say and he nods, looking at me, trying to focus on my face. One of the medics is cleaning the dirt out of the wounds on his legs and I turn to him.

"At least he's not deaf. How are the legs?"

"Just blast burns, sir. They'll take a bit of time to heal, but he'll be O.K."

The 2I.C. has just finished radioing through for a chopper and turns round in his chair.

"Could you have a word with the O.C.?" I say to him. "All that bull was totally unnecessary. If I talk to him, I'll just get myself into trouble."

"Don't worry, I'll deal with it. God, the man has about as much knowledge of man-management as a duck."

"What happened?"

"When he was coming in from patrol, he saw an Army torch lying on the road just outside the gate. So he cleared the area, got everyone into the base, put a line on it and then led the line through the gate and shut it after him. He then pulled and the torch exploded."

"How come the burns then?"

"Well, the torch must have rolled by the gate and there is a two-inch gap at the bottom. When it blew, the blast went under the gate and hit Sgt. Denny."

"So in fact he did all the right things and was just unlucky. He wasn't being incompetent at all. Does the O.C. know all this?"

"No, he didn't bother to find out all the facts before he hit the roof."

"Silly cunt. God, that man!"

These last few days have not been too good as far as the O.C. is concerned, but what really gets to me is that he doesn't know that he is putting everybody's backs up. Just wanders around in his own little world hiding behind his rank. To hell with him!

1800 hrs. July 1976

They blew up a Tom
Yesterday,
Snatched the life out
Of him,
Spread it over the
Square.

It only seems like yesterday since I was on the helicopter going the other way on R. and R. Now I'm flying back into Crossmaglen, seeing the familiar landscape, thinking tactics and wondering what is in store for me after the Battalion's success the day I left for England a week ago. An OP couldn't believe their eyes when they were presented with a carload of gunmen, obviously on a first-time mission. Having managed to hit one, the ensuing chase brought a crop of five complete with weapons. But underneath the jubilation at having at last captured some of the opposition, was the disappointment at the fact that they were amateurs out on a badly organised murder operation aimed at some local Prots.

It's annoying for us down in Crossmaglen, because the Company that has had no action at all get everything handed to them, whilst we carry on tip-toeing around in the most dangerous area of Ulster. No doubt someone is going to get a medal. The helicopter completes its final approach and we touch down on the helipad, climb out and run to the back gate.

"Hello boss, back to the hub of the Universe, the centre of entertainment, the one, the only X.M.G." Sgt. Denny greets me, now almost fully recovered from his burns and back on duty.

"Hi there. Isn't this just a lovely place. I've been waiting all week for this moment. Like fuck I have."

"Well, it's good to have you back, the O.C. has been driving us all up the wall."

"Oh no, not back to all that."

We carried on discussing the problems of the camp and the situation on the ground, as we made our way to the Mess for a brew and for me to drop my kit and get into uniform. There have only been some minor contacts while I've been away, nothing much to shout about, just odd shots from over the border and some low-velocity rounds fired at the OP.

My little cupboard seems strangely welcoming and it is frightening just how easy it is to slip into the routine, forgetting the interlude of R. and R.

"Pte. Anson shot himself in the foot the other day." I look up in astonishment.

"How on earth did that happen?"

"We were following up on a shooting, entered a house and he tripped over the carpet. Bang, one hole through foot."

"Clever, very clever." As if we haven't got enough on our plate without clowns shooting themselves. Whatever next.

"O.K. Jimmy, give me the good news, when am I out?"

"0400 hrs tomorrow morning, an area foot patrol. You walk out, get picked up by chopper tomorrow night and lifted across to the Cullyhanna area, and so on for the following three nights."

"What, three night pick-ups?"

"Yep."

"Wonderful."

I hate night pick-ups, because some of the pilots insist on putting on their landing lights and illuminating the entire area. The best pilots seem to be the Royal Navy guys. At least they try and fly as tactically as possible with the ancient Wessex. So, for three night pick-ups sitting there naked in the floodlight, my insides are turning to water again already.

"How are the lads doing?"

"Pretty good. There are a couple who are real dozy still, but the rest are pretty switched on."

The dark shape of the helicopter is getting bigger and I'm standing here in the middle of the L.Z. hoping the pilot is not going to switch on his landing lights. We seem to be lucky and have drawn a good one because he comes straight in on my torchlight and puts the metal monster down just in front of me. The lads pile on board and I grab the spare headset and tell the pilot where I want to be dropped off, as I've decided to change the L.Z. He seems quite happy and wheels the aircraft around the night sky with apparent abandon. Must be a Navy pilot.

This is the second pick-up that has gone very smoothly and I'm thinking that if the rest of the patrol goes off like this, it is going to be a good week. Flight time is only four minutes and we descend into the dark field, land and bale out and wait while the helicopter lifts and flies off into the night. The noise has melted away, the silence only broken by the sound of the radio and rustlings of animals in the bushes and hedgerows.

"Cpl. Menzies and Cpl. Edge, over here." There is a scrabbling sound and they move across and drop on the ground beside me.

"We'll move across to the mountain and make a firm base for the night up in the rocks. Tomorrow will be soon enough to decide which way to go. I'll lead, then Cpl. Edge and you Bill bring up the rear. O.K."

"Right boss."

"Move out in five minutes."

The summer night sky is fairly light which makes moving around fairly easy and as we approach the mountains, the hedges and fields become bigger and blackthorn gives way to dry-stone walls, making crossing easier. The mountains are on the eastern edge of our area and borders with C. Company over in Forkhill. The boundaries between areas are always difficult to patrol and there must be good communications between the Companies involved otherwise there could be an accident. Seeing a group of people strolling around at night armed to the teeth could be somewhat nerve-racking if you're not expecting them.

It's tiring work climbing up the side of the mountain, and takes longer than I expected. However, we finally find a suitable spot and drop into a natural hollow about twenty feet deep and one hundred feet across, surrounded on all sides by rock parapets. Perfect.

With the guns placed to give all-round defence and a rota system organised, the Toms can crawl into little folds in the ground and get a few hours sleep before the dawn. We're about three hundred feet up and the whole area is visible. Away to the south, the lights of Dundalk in the Republic twinkle in the clear air. To the north, only odd lights here and there break up the dark brooding landscape.

A slight breeze ruffles the coarse mountain grass, blowing through the tree branches, gently caressing the leaves, slightly stirring them in their sleep. It is a time to sit and reflect on the beauty of the countryside, on the unspoilt wildlife that abounds and flourishes. The sight of a fox dashing through the undergrowth, brilliant red brush streaming behind and, on a night like this, to watch with fascination the meanderings of the badger on his nightly forage. Beneath the brash exterior of the Toms is a natural sensitivity that is shown in their expressions as they watch the night-time parade. Only recently, on a patrol, one of them found a young marsh warbler suffering from exhaustion and seemingly incapable of fending for itself. The Tom concerned emptied a pouch of his pack, filled it with grass and popped the bird in. For two days he carried the bird around before we got back to base. He then cared for the bird until it was well enough to set free. All this from the crudest, hardest guy in the platoon.

Sitting here thinking these thoughts, looking out over the most troubled part of the province, it seems so unreal, just a dream from which we will soon wake and find ourselves back in Aldershot. It is so unfair that all this beauty should be wasted on these people. Back to reality and I check the guns and the Toms manning them.

"O.K. up here?"

"Great sir, it's a fuckin' good place," comes the whispered reply.

"Fine, just don't go to sleep, you'll be relieved in an hour." He just nods and continues scanning the countryside. They all seem quite happy, feeling relatively safe up here in the rocks with a good view.

Getting out of the camp is becoming a scary business as we all feel now that the possibility of a booby trap close in is very real and becoming more likely with the passing days. I check every gap in the hedges for trip-wires before going through and look for disturbed ground. The further away from base we get the more easily we breathe, which explains the relaxed attitude of the Toms as they close their eyes up here on the mountain. I make my way down to where Smith has found a little nook and curl up close by so that I can hear the radio transmissions. Pulling my smock around me I try and get some sleep; it's going to be an early start again, as soon as dawn breaks. Before I go to sleep, the day's happenings flit through my mind and I can see again the face of the woman we stopped on a routine V.C.P. She was a Prot and had her son with her. As soon as we stopped her she started ranting on about how we should be getting the gunmen instead of stopping innocent people on the road. She then went on to say that her son had been tortured by the I.R.A. and shot nine times in the thighs. To prove the point, she made the poor bugger show us the bullet wounds in his legs. The feeling of shame I had at the time was indescribable. Shame, not for myself, but for the fact that I was a member of the so-called "human race". Why do people enjoy inflicting pain on others? With that question burning in my mind, I close my eyes.

The last night pick-up dropped us off just before dawn about a thousand metres to the east of Monog on the other side of the hill, to enable us to patrol back in and clear that side of the town, before returning to base. Monog looks no different in the flattering light of dawn, perched on the edge of the hill, grubby houses like dirty smudges against the fresh green of the fields. Beyond, catching the first light of day, Crossmaglen. The church over to our right dominating the town; the church, the local icon, the local salve to a wounded collective conscience; the church, rich, impressive, the excuse for barbarity and the salvation from it.

The town square, plainly visible over the top of the tatty buildings, the centre stage of the eternal play, with the base occupying the best seats in the house. Oh well, take a deep breath and start moving on down the hill towards the village and trust everyone is asleep today.

The dogs hear us coming and start their barking, declaring our exact location by the intensity of the sound. I may be a dog lover with one of my own, but when my life is at risk they become a hazard. From the yard of a small farm comes the high-pitched squeal of an animal in pain and the barking dies away. Suddenly the whole village is quiet save the whimpering of the injured animal. One of the Toms appears from the yard with an evil grin on his face.

"Won't have any more trouble, boss," he says and creeps away to join his patrol.

We wander around the village for a little while, peeking in at windows, digging around unlocked outhouses and generally being nosey. It's great at this time in the morning with the place deserted, everyone in bed, some sleeping, others in the process of creating more mouths to feed. Monog, a seedy collection of unkempt dwellings, rusty cars and hate-filled people. Not exactly Ulster's best tourist attraction. Bored with poking our noses around, we make our way over the fields and across towards the Dundalk road, to put an early morning V.C.P. on it by the school.

The Toms are getting restless now to get back in and have a good breakfast after the past few days of compo rations. It would be nice to have a wash and shave too. We look more like a bunch of tramps, with filthy boots and denims, and stubble-covered chins.

"O.K. Cpl. Edge, move off back to camp and go firm at the junction with the square. As soon as you are firm, we'll move through you and in at the front gate."

The first patrol walks slowly up the road toward the square whilst we wait here and cover their rear. It looks as if it will be a nice day.

Having had breakfast, washed, shaved and rescued my burning denims from the drier before the base goes up in flames, it is time to check that all the Toms are safely tucked away. Apart from eating and cleaning weapons, sleep is the most important item, because a tired Tom is a danger to himself as well as the rest of the patrol.

The bunkhouse is long and narrow, with between eight and ten

Toms to each room. Communal living with a vengeance, and it is surprising that more fights don't break out.

Looking into the rooms, I can just make out the green humped shapes of occupied sleeping bags on some bunks and on others the quiet sight of a Tom writing home or gently cleaning his rifle. The walls are festooned with naked women cut out of the more risqué magazines of European origin, together with posters and drawings of rubber ducks.

It may be a job, but the living and working conditions would be condemned by any health authority. Earlier on in the tour, due to the bad weather and various other problems, we had been unable to get the rubbish out of the base and it became worse than any Bombay slum. Disinfectant was spread around every day to combat the possibility of disease and the smell of this mixed with the smell of rotting food became an overpowering accompaniment to the already miserably cramped conditions.

Leaving the bunkhouse, I drop in and see Sgt. Denny, whose private little cubby-hole is even smaller than mine. Rubber ducks are not only all over the outside, they are also inside. That plus the familiar "Quack" greeting that has now become the platoon's verbal mascot, makes the whole place just a little bizarre.

"How's it going Jimmy?"

"O.K. boss, just getting a little pissed off with our leader."

"Oh, what's he been doing now?"

"He wants me to take a bloke out from Brigade on my next patrol. One of those *'I've been to Crossmaglen'* things." I don't say a word. It seems that this place attracts the day-trippers from desk jobs in search of a thrill so that they can go back to England and say, *"Of course, I've been to Crossmaglen."* They are time-wasters and put lives at risk more often than not. If they want to come down here they should do a tour, perhaps that would cure them.

We even had a chopper-load of strippers flown down to see the troops, who were all on the ground protecting them from the possibility of another attack on the aircraft carrying them. So all they saw were the cooks and a handful of half-asleep Toms who had just come off a four-day patrol.

"Well, there are going to be a lot more of them coming before the tour is over," I say at last.

"I guess you're right, but can't you have a word with the O.C. anyway and see if there is anything we can do about it?"

"I'll try, but I doubt it will do any good."

"O.K. boss, now if you would like to fuck off, I can get some sleep."

"Cheers."

I leave him quacking and wander round the base like a lost soul. There is nothing stirring at this time of the morning except a dozing Sgt. Major in the Ops Room and the cook beginning breakfast. Not even the sound of a helicopter disturbs the quiet and I want to stay awake as long as possible to enjoy this private time, before the bustle of base life resumes in earnest for another day.

My reverie is disturbed by the sound of panting and running feet, and round the corner of the bunkhouse comes one of the Toms, dressed in plastic waterproofs, on his daily weight-reducing jog around the base. Someone computed that one mile was equal to about thirty laps, avoiding scaffolding, plastic rubbish bags, other people walking round the camp and sundry other obstacles.

"Come on you fat fucker, run!" I shout encouragement and miss with a kick at his retreating rotund behind.

"You can't crack me," he shouts, panting out of sight.

"Lunch is ready, if you want any, sir."

I wake to the horrific sight of the Sgt. Major's grinning face outlined in the door of my bunk.

"What time is it?"

"1300 and if you don't come quick, J.C.B. is going to have the lot." His face disappears and only the dismembered cackle remains. My head feels woolly and my eyes don't focus too well. It may be daylight outside but in here it's black. I switch on the light and search for my denims and boots, get dressed, stagger out into the narrow corridor and head for the noise in the Mess.

It seems there is standing room only at the table today, but a couple are just about finishing, so by the time I get back up from the cookhouse with my scoff, there will be an empty place.

The conversation is all shop, as can be expected, so it is a relief when the place empties and there is only myself, my Sgt. and the C.S.M. The two of them are busy discussing admin, to which I am only listening with half an ear. I'm still half-asleep and don't particularly want to wake up just yet, trying to cling on to the dream I was having about naked women and South Sea Islands before I was so rudely interrupted.

"I see your boss is alert and happy," says the C.S.M.

"You want to see him when he's asleep."

"Fuck off you two, I'm communing with my inner being." Derisive gestures and quacks.

"I reckon he's cracking, what do you think Sgt. Denny?"

"For sure, for sure." It goes on and on and I just sit and let it go over my head, brain not capable of witty repartee.

"Enough, enough, I give up. What do you want from me?"

"Someone to run the film this afternoon, boss."

"Well that's not so bad. Could be a lot worse. O.K. will do."

The next patrol is at 2200 hrs tonight, so there is plenty of time to get sorted after the film and at least the guys will have something to take their minds off the five days to come.

I finish my food, lean back, yawn, stretch and start thinking what to do or rather what has to be done in the next few hours before it's patrol time again. Work out a route, checking the route map in the Int. cell to make sure that I don't go over any old ground and follow previous trails. Organise the rations; sort out the equipment required and whatever else needs to be done.

"When are you out, Jimmy?"

"1900 hrs the chopper comes in."

"I'll run the film at about 1400 hrs then, give your guys a chance to see it before they go out."

He nods, gets up and goes off whistling to himself. The C.S.M. lights another cigarette, leans back and sips his tea between clouds of smoke.

"You're looking pale Sar'nt Major. You should get out on the ground, get some fresh air into those decimated lungs of yours."

"Fuck off sir, I'll leave all that stuff to you lot. I'm too old for that sort of thing."

"True, true," I say and dodge the lump of butter tossed at my head.

"You know sir, you're not at all like an officer," he says.

"Oh, and what is an officer like?"

"You know what I mean. You're easier to get along with than most of them, even though you are a wanker."

"Thanks very much, you're not bad, for a wrinkled prune, yourself."

The O.C. comes in and interrupts our slanging match going on about patrol states, what we are going to do next, admin and such like. Looking at him while he talks, I'm not listening to him, just thinking what a strange guy he is. He seems to live in a world of his own, in a self-contained cell that is impossible to penetrate. To me, he has always been generous and we get on well, but to the Toms he is the "O.C." and to him they are just things that are there to get the job done. He may be good at paperwork, but man-management is something that he knows nothing of, which is very sad.

He and the C.S.M. are talking about the next patrol to take over the O'Meath V.C.P. on the border and a nice little number for a week, although there is always the danger that it will get blown up again. I was there in June and it was a great week just relaxing, searching cars, watching the Olympics on the T.V. and shooting the odd rats that roam around the accommodation. Wouldn't mind another week there, it certainly is a cushy number, with its own little helipad and the beauty of Carlingford Lough.

"What do you think, Tony?" The O.C. is talking to me and I'm not listening.

"I'm sorry I was miles away."

The discussion is about some reorganisation that the O.C. has dreamed up, and continues for the next fifteen minutes until I excuse myself to put on the film in the cookhouse.

I know what it is before the sound carries. The ground shakes a split second before the ear-splitting crunch of the explosion drowns out the sound track of the film. For a moment, there is stunned inaction, then chaos.

"Mortars!" shouts someone, but there is no sound of falling masonry.

"Shut up and get out and get your weapons," I shout, feeling a dread within me.

Outside in the compound, Toms are racing around as if their balls have been cut off.

"Listen you cunts, just calm down and get to your stand-to positions. Don't run around like fucking idiots."

The only place I'm going to find out what has happened is in the Ops Room, so that's where I'm headed. By the pale faces I know it is bad and it has happened to one of my patrols. Just half an hour ago I sent a patrol out to secure the area around the helipad because some top R.A.F. officer wanted to have some practice runs into the helipad. The patrol were just on their way in.

"It's a bomb in the square Tony, one dead."

One Tom dead in the square. One Tom sacrificed on the altar of political ineptitude. One Tom publicly executed in the name of freedom.

"How?" I ask, numb.

"We don't know yet, the stand-by section are out there and the Saracen to pick up the body."

I can't stay in the Ops Room any longer, the rage and emotion in me are on the point of bursting out. I just wander around the camp, checking the OPs, getting myself under control. It's happened just as I thought, a bomb close in, right under our noses so that it has maximum effect on morale. The only saving grace is that it only took out one of the patrol and not the whole lot. God how I hate this place!

The C.S.M. is coming towards me.

"They're bringing him in now sir, and the patrol should be in shortly. It's Pte. Borucki."

"Thanks Sar'nt Major. I'll be along in a minute."

Pull yourself together Clarke, you've got to sort out the patrol when they come in and make them angry in order to chase the shock and horror away and get them working efficiently again.

The front gate opens and the Saracen drives in bearing its pathetic burden. The C.Sgt. is ready with the body bag and it doesn't take long to remove the dog tags and other personal possessions. There is not much left of the right side of his body. Once in the bag, he is just another memory written in blood on the streets and consciences of Ulster, soon to be forgotten. The patrol comes in looking ashen-faced and shaken.

"O.K. you guys, into the stand-by room." I reckon that if I can isolate them I can get through to them.

"Now listen to me. It's happened and that's that. If you don't want to go the same way, then you had better pull yourselves together. As soon as you leave this room you're back on duty, so if you want to fall apart, do it now and get it over with."

The harsh words seem to have the desired effect and those on the verge of tears choke them back and bring themselves under control. "Now, tell me what happened."

Cpl. Edge, the patrol commander at the time, speaks. "We had finished the stake-out and were coming in by the square. I led the way up to the corner and started up towards the front gate. Borucki was behind me. As I turned around I could see him crouching down on the corner to cover the next bloke round when the bicycle that was leaning against the wall blew up." His voice was shaking but grew stronger as he recounted the events.

"O.K. Cpl. Edge, when you're ready the O.C. wants a full report. Remember lads, as soon as you go through this door, you're back on duty." With that I leave them to it.

Dead at eighteen. Not an accident or natural catastrophe, but publicly murdered, snuffed out before he has the chance to even know what all this is about, before he has known what life is. That makes two now, because the other guy who was blown up, in Sgt. Donne's patrol, died after a week. What did they die for? The recurring question that defies answer.

The town was flooded with patrols after the incident and they are now bringing people in for questioning. Frightened people with their chests heaving and eyes wide in terror. They know that we only need the slightest excuse to beat them or shoot them and all the Toms would dearly love to do the latter.

Outside, down at the square, a B.B.C. news camera crew are filming the remains like the vultures on carrion. I would dearly love to know how they managed to get down here so soon after the explosion. Fucking news teams! What do they know?

"The training is over. From now on everything you do will be for real. The next rounds you face will be live ones, headed your way with only one aim. Excuse the pun. Where we are going, the I.R.A. don't attack unless they can virtually guarantee a kill. Whether it's a bomb or bullets. There's the possibility that some of you will not be coming back."

Words from the boss. Words from me. Words you hope they'll listen to. Words that mean you and you and maybe you are probably going to die. Melodramatic words nobody wants to hear. But somehow the reality has to be faced.

"Can't we shoot them first, boss?" Laughter.

"If you can see them, you can shoot them. Just remember, you are still bound by the conditions of the yellow card. That means whatever happens, they always fire first. Whether they actually do or not, nobody will ever know. Get my meaning? As far as this platoon is concerned, anyone seen with a gun is fair game. As far as everybody else is concerned, we do everything by the yellow card." Nods of eager assent. Death in the eyes. Blood-lust. Training paying off. No, not just training. Conditioning. Twenty-five controlled thugs looking faintly absurd in their civilian clothes, ready for their pre-embarkation leave.

"I don't need to remind anyone that going A.W.O.L. at this stage of the game is just about the worst thing you can

do. From now on you are on active service. Don't ever forget that. For the next five months your rifle will never leave your sight and walks in the country will be with pockets full of live ammunition. Anyone any questions?"

"Yes. When can we leave? The train is due any minute."

"Carry on like that Rankin and I'm sure I can find you some extra guard duties." Jeers and boos from the lads. Smiles from the silent platoon staff. "O.K. That's it. The next time you'll see myself and your section commanders will be in Crossmaglen."

"Keep your head down sir."

"Why bother?"

"Watch the crap-hats."

Random remarks tossed out by Toms racing out of the door to catch the train. A minute and I'm alone with the section commanders and Jimmy my platoon Sgt.

"What do you reckon? Are they going to be all right?"

"No problems boss. A couple are a little shaky, but there's nothing like the odd round or two to get people moving."

"Let's hope it's not the odd bomb or two."

"Any problems with your sections?" This to the section commanders.

"Borucki's a bit dodgy in my crew, but he's a good radio op. Apart from that they're fine."

"Mine too. No problems."

"All sounds very convincing. Hope you're right. That place is a death-trap and most of these guys have never seen a riot or experienced a gun battle." My mind quickly reeling back to the Shankill in 1973. Images of darkened streets. The helicopter with its searchlight. The O.C. diving for cover and Hookey and I standing in the middle of the road directing gunfire.

"Sorry. What did you say?"

"I just asked if you were happy with your patrol set-up."
Rueful smile at Jimmy who asked the question.

"Fait accompli, I think."

"Fate a what, boss?" he says grinning.

"At least the gunners are good. But Old and Sinclair? I didn't think you hated me that much. Jesus."

"Just thought they'd learn much more with you boss."

"Boy, the survival instinct is really coming out now."

"As always. Somebody needs to be around to pick up the pieces."

"Cheers you bastards." The banter continues. It has to. Resign yourself to the fact that you could be just some messy cold meat lying in a mortuary somewhere. Just don't let it hurt. That's all. If I'm going, let's go out with a bang. Get spread out all over the place. The hell with losing an arm or a leg.

"Right. That's it. Ferry leaves in two days. Time to go and fuck yourselves rotten. You may never get it again."

It's all over in a very short time and we're back to the routine of patrols, guards, searches and more patrols. One of the young R.U.C. constables we have at the base has been complaining of our treatment of suspects and so has had to be put straight about a few things. In the three months we've been here, this guy hasn't ventured outside the camp, just sits around all day collecting overtime and extra Crossmaglen allowances. Nice work if you can get it.

Standing by the back gate, rifle cocked, pack on, and face covered with smears of cam-cream, thinking of places where booby traps might be hidden on our route out to the L.Z., 600 metres to the south of the base.

"Everybody ready?" Nods of assent, though not at all enthusiastic. "Let's go."

Whenever I'm really scared, I get light-headed and something inside takes over and moves my body round. This is one of those occasions with me seeming to be outside myself watching the goings on with more than a little apprehension.

No matter how good you are at feeling for trip-wires, there always comes the moment you dread, when you have to put the first foot through the gap in the hedge and the other, popping out on the other side, hoping they haven't gone one better and put a pressure pad on the other side. Once through, I sit there shaking in the dark, willing myself on to the next obstacle. I go first because I know that if I do hit a wire I won't realise it and will probably be killed outright instead of badly maimed. I've heard of some Toms saying that if they get zapped and dismembered and are still alive, they want to be shot rather than be a cabbage. Me too!

The patrol goes quietly enough, with the darkness sneering at my fear and soon we are at the L.Z. and the welcoming sound of a chopper descending to transport us away to a safer part of the area.

0430 hrs. August 1976

The end
Of the tour
Is just
The beginning.

"The Royal Marines are due in a couple of days..." The O.C. droning on at me. I'm tired and dirty having just got back in from a ten-day patrol. Bed. I need my bed and some sleep. There is also the constant pain in my gut from eating this crappy compo food. Sleep and a good meal then I'll be fine. I don't need to listen to this shit about the Marines.

"Can't it wait till later Major?"

"It needs to be gone through very thoroughly."

"I can appreciate that. But at this moment I can't concentrate on a thing. Let me have time for a sleep." It seems as if he is going to be stupid and insist on doing the briefing right now. A look, then a shrug of the shoulders.

"O.K. Let's have as many people as you can get together for 1000 hrs." Thank Christ for that. He saunters off to the Mess or bed. I head for the Ops Room and a check on the patrol programme for the rest of the week.

It's strange walking round the camp at this time in the morning. Lights are on as the dawn struggles to begin another day. Toms walking around in a daze, some through exhaustion, others because they haven't woken up yet. From the Ops Room occasional detached voices from the intercom passing routine messages. Look in through the door and there is the C.S.M. sitting dozing at the desk whilst the radio op listens to the set and plays patience.

"Come on you lazy old wrinkled prune you," says I. He jerks awake and stares bleary-eyed.

"Oh shit. You back already. Why don't you just stay out there and give us all a rest."

"Sgt. Major, you say the sweetest things. But who else would keep you sane?"

"True. True," says he, rubbing his eyes. "Hey, you don't look so good."

"Thanks. That's all I need after the O.C. trying to give a briefing on the hand-over."

"So he's been at it again, has he? Don't worry, we've got most of the admin side worked out."

"I thought you might have. I'm off to the pit. Got to have some sleep." Guess I'll have food after. Right now the eyes are beginning to close and the brain doing abstract somersaults.

The pit, the pit, my kingdom for the pit! The last ten days in the OP my stomach has been really bad. It's been coming on for the past month or so and now I noticed I'm shitting blood and it really hurts. Constant need to take a shit on patrol. Dive behind a hedge and let the blood out that I feel sloshing around inside.

Perhaps the Sgt. Major was right. Maybe I'm overlooking my own health. And for what? Guess I'll take a trip to see the M.O. tomorrow. He'll sort me out with some pills and I can get back to finish the last week and a half of the tour.

"You back already?" The 2I.C. doing his bit to make me feel welcome. "Place was very peaceful for the last few days. I suppose your crazy Sgt. is back too?"

"What a welcome. I didn't know you missed us so much. What the fuck are you doing up at this time? Rather unusual to say the least. Shouldn't you be catching up on your ten hours sleep?"

"Piss off, Clarke."

"Gladly." This time I really will get to bed. Any decisions I need to make can be made in the morning. Right now I sleep.

The pain in the gut wakes me up. What the fuck's the time? Jesus! Only nine o'clock. Sod it, this pain is not too clever and I noticed more blood last night. Right. That's it. Today I see the M.O. The Major is going to be pleased! Sod the Major!

Crawl out of bed. Find something to put on over my emaciated dirty frame and stagger to the washroom. Get some of the filth off. The Major is just coming out of his bunk. Oh shit! Really could do without seeing him just now.

"Morning Major."

"Are you going to be ready in time for the briefing at ten?" he says. No "good morning," I notice.

"Actually there is something I want to tell you." He looks at me a little coldly. "I need to see the M.O. Been having a bit of trouble with the stomach over the last patrol. I want to make sure it's cleared up for the next one."

"You'd better get yourself a helicopter ordered and get back here as soon as possible." With that he walks off.

Well. No problem there. Get washed and do as he says. Get that helicopter down here A.S.A.P. Scoot into the Mess and contact the Ops Room by tannoy and order up the helicopter. By the time I've showered, eaten and got my kit together, the sound of a Gazelle sweeping overhead, permeates the building.

"Chopper here for you sir." The voice from the Ops Room through the tannoy.

"Thanks. I'm on my way." Race down the stairs. Out of the back gate and towards the Gazelle as it settles on the helipad. Within a few seconds we are airborne as I busy myself fastening the seat belt. Crossmaglen disappears under the aircraft and we are away.

The flight to Bessbrook doesn't take very long and we are soon swinging down between the anti-rocket screens onto the helipad beside the other parked helicopters. Land. A cheery wave to the pilot and it's off to roust out the M.O. No mean feat in this rambling place they call Battalion Headquarters.

Up to the gate and go through the usual procedures, then follow the signs to the M.I. Room.

"Morning sir!" Greetings from a cheery medical orderly.

"Morning. Is the M.O. around? He knows I'm coming."

"Up in the Mess, sir. I'll give him a buzz. Won't be long."

With that he disappears into the office and I sit down. Mind into neutral and stare at the cream and brown walls. Must have dozed off, because the next thing I know, John, the M.O., is staring into my face.

"Well, Tony. What can we do for you?" I go through the problem feeling slightly embarrassed and then feel a nagging doubt as I catch the look on his face.

Five minutes and a check-up later.

"I think I'm going to send you to hospital. I don't like the look of that."

"Well!" Intelligent as ever. "What do you think the problem is?"

"That's what I want the hospital to find out. I'll get some transport laid on to take you up to Belfast."

"You'd also better tell the O.C. He's expecting me back for a patrol tonight."

"No chance! You're finished for the rest of the tour. Anyway it's only a week."

"Fine. You can talk to him. I'll just tell my platoon Sgt."

Just like that. Tour finished. No more Crossmaglen. Shit. I left my great big china mug in the camp. Bet that vanishes!

4. Death and a New Life

1430 hrs. 26ᵗʰ July 1977

Dear God
Let me die
It would be
A blessed relief

"If I operate I'll kill you," he says looking everywhere but into my eyes.

"I'm dying anyway so what difference will it make, except I won't be in agony anymore," I croak scornfully, barely able to speak as the knife-like pain rips through my shredded guts and another gout of blood pours onto the already soaked sheets. I see the wings on his sleeve and feel betrayed. "You're a Para for Christ's sake." I'm angry now and my voice is stronger. "Show some backbone. Operate."

Still he doesn't look at me, just lays a hand on my shoulder, gets up and walks away, freeing me to see the view out of the window of the Intensive Nursing Unit of the Queen Elizabeth Military Hospital Woolwich, across a narrow car park to the cemetery beyond. Ironic isn't it that I'm in the *'no-hopers ward'* along with brain-injured soldiers, waiting to die, looking out at my final resting place.

Another bout of agonizing pain racks my already emaciated body. I'm curled up in the foetal position with a PICC (Peripherally Inserted Central Catheter) line up my arm into the top of my heart, two feeding tubes into the other arm praying for the next shot of pethidine. It comes every four hours but the relief only lasts for sixty minutes before the agony begins again.

Day and night, hour after hour, day after day.

What goes in at the top comes straight out through my arse.

"Will you have something to eat Captain Clarke," a bright-eyed, immaculately starched QA nurse asks me.

"Eat? You have to be kidding. My guts are already shredded." My disdainful comment comes out as a barely decipherable noise.

"The Colonel says you need to eat. Try some chicken vol-au-vent."

'Chicken fucking vol-au-vent? Has the whole fucking world gone completely fucking mad?" I'm thinking. Well, maybe by the look on the nurse's face I'm speaking out loud, but then I can barely speak. Doesn't matter anyway. *I'm dying you stupid bitch and you want me to chow down on chicken fucking vol-au-vent? Is this a hospital or a fucking abattoir?'* Somewhere down the ward one of the brain smashed squaddies moans incomprehensibly, the sounds growing louder and louder which sets off a chorus with the other mangled former human beings.

"Morphine. That's what I want."

"What did you say? Was that a yes? Vol-au-vent for lunch?"

I try to summon up the strength to shout, but it comes out as a hoarse whisper.

"No. Not fucking chicken fucking vol-au-vents, fucking morphine."

"Not yet," she says icily. "Another three hours."

"I'll be dead in three fucking hours."

She hears that but doesn't answer, just looks confused, messes with the chart and walks briskly away with a parting, "Chicken vol-au-vent it is."

'Cheers. The condemned doesn't even get a choice, just chicken fucking vol-au-fucking-vent.' If it wasn't so desperately pathetic and unbelievably screwed up, this whole experience would be a Tommy Cooper comedy routine.

But it's not.

I'm dying.

The last of my life sustaining fluids are draining away no matter how much they pour into me. I can feel the poisons seeping from my gut into my body cavity and don't understand why I'm still conscious.

Oh yes, the pain. That's why. The constant mind shattering pain and nobody can hear me scream because I'm so weak and emaciated my eyesight is going and my voice is almost silent and I barely have the strength to raise my head.

It would be easy to just slip away, jack it all in and become just another Northern Ireland statistic. Just another forgotten casualty of a war nobody will call a war.

They're all here, the statistics.

The burned; the brain dead.

The teenage bodies once full of life and energy, gloriously vain and self-centred, full of piss and vinegar with muscles to match, now twitching screaming moaning pathetic macabre caricatures of vibrant youthful beauty.

Every bump in the road he screams and his wife cries non-stop. And when he stops screaming in agony he sobs and apologises to me.

"Sorry sir. Can't help it. Sorry sir."

"It's O.K. son," I mutter feeling useless and a total fraud, my problems a mere shadow to his horror. He was driving a Saracen when it was firebombed in Belfast. The only way out was through the flames to the back door, a human torch screaming all the way as he watched the flesh drip from his hands, felt it sliding off his face and then his body as his clothes lit up like a roman candle. God knows how long it was before he lost consciousness. But now every lurch of the ambulance carrying us from the RAF Hospital in Brize Norton to the Queen Elizabeth Military Hospital in Woolwich, was as if he was reliving the agony and the nightmare all over again.

And his impossibly young wife can only look at the cooked shell of her young, once handsome husband, and cry with an indescribable loneliness and grief.

His agony makes my pain seems so insignificant and I hate him for that. I hate him for making me feel like I want to shoot him just to stop him from screaming, but it goes on and on the entire journey to London. Sometimes he lapses into unconsciousness and I can breath easier and concentrate on my own silent world of crushing pain with just the sobbing of the young wife echoing my disconnected thoughts.

*And then the ambulance brakes hard and corners fast,
throwing us around like rag dolls even though we're strapped
to our stretchers.*
   And the screaming starts again.

It was only six days ago but it seems like a lifetime.

It is a lifetime; my lifetime, every precious moment a jewel to be savoured no matter how terrifying. I wonder what happened to that soldier. Is he the one screaming and moaning at the end of the ward calling for '*Susan*'? Or did he just die like so many others. Even in the five days I've been here, I've seen the curtain close around a few beds and the covered gurneys slide out and away, the nurses pretending nothing happened.

'You can tell us. We're grown-ups. We know anyway. It doesn't matter. None of it matters. We don't matter, that's very clear. Everything by the book. Never question a senior rank. Just shut up and die like a man so we can get on with.... With what?'

Get on with surviving. That's what. Somehow I have this thought that I'm going to survive no matter what they say. It's the '*fuck you I'm a Para*' side of my character, the side that is going to do the opposite of what anybody says. If I'm told I can't, I say I can. It comes from my Grandmother, my mother's mother. The trouble is I'm dying, I know I am and don't have to be told, but I'm hanging onto the edge of the cliff of life by my fingernails. I've got them dug in so far it'll take a crow bar to prise them loose, but I have to stay awake. I can't slip off into that blessed twilight of semi-consciousness because if I do I may never come back, just drift into the permanent darkness of death.

Yesterday the Padre stopped by to offer whatever comfort he could, but his eyes told me that he knew that the abstract idea of paradise beyond death was no comfort to a young dying soldier.

'Goddam it I'm only twenty-seven years old. I have a wife, two daughters and another on the way, what the hell's going to happen to them.'

A passing nurse looks at me strangely and I wonder if I shouted that or just thought it. My gut cramps up again and I know I'm screaming but the sound is a pathetic whimper as another gout of blood splashes on the sheets.

'How much can a body take before it just gives up and stops working?' I idly think as the spasm gives way to just routine agony that's nothing to speak of in comparison. Every moment is simply about the pain. My entire existence is centred on the rotting diseased intestine falling apart inside me, there's very little time to think about anything else except for the sixty minutes of pethidine bliss when I can let my mind drift to the past. There is no future so why dwell on that?

Just the past.

TAC HQ Bessbrook, South Armagh, 11ᵗʰ August 1976 and I'm in borrowed civvies with a 9mm Browning tucked into my waistband sitting in the back seat of a Q car with a driver and one soldier riding 'shotgun'. Apparently there are no helicopters available and the MO wants me admitted to the Military wing of Musgrave Park Hospital in Belfast ASAP. So the only choice is to drive.

I'm shaking my head in disbelief.

For the past four months we've been patrolling on foot or been dropped off by helicopter, because driving vehicles around is too fucking dangerous.

So what do they do?

Load me into a Q car, drive forty miles and expect nothing to happen. That's why we have two Remington pump action shotguns and two submachine guns not to mention the 9mm Brownings.

What the hell, the pain in my gut is going to keep my mind busy and I really don't give a shit anymore. I think I'd welcome a gun battle right now and get it all over with instead of this constant nagging pain. And then there's the old adage, 'every soldier knows when he not coming back from war'. *Borucki knew he was going to die.*

How long ago was that? Seems like a lifetime, but it was

only a few days ago.

Jesus. Another week and a half and he would have been home, safe.

There's a VCP ahead and we all get jittery in the car. Here we are in civvies armed to the teeth and the soldiers manning the VCP are supposed to let us through? But our driver has done this before and we're through with a nod and on our way.

The rest of the journey is a blur; the countryside giving way to the grey houses of Belfast and it's raining again. The car pulls up at the checkpoint to the Military Wing of the Musgrave Park Hospital and after we are screened, we drive to the entrance and I hand over my weapons, climb out and walk slowly into the reception area. My head is swimming, the pain in my bowel constant and nauseating. They're expecting me, the QAs here are efficient, no nonsense. They deal with gunshot wounds, blast injuries, burns, everything. They've seen it all and then some, so they are pretty dismissive of my little complaint.

I don't blame them, I feel like a fraud.

I wasn't shot, or blown up, but the effects are the same. Just inside my body.

I'm shown deference because I'm a Para Officer, and before long I'm lying on my side in an examination room with a doctor shoving a stainless steel tube the size of the Mersey Tunnel up my arse. I'm gripping a nurse's hand and the pain is indescribable. I squeeze her hand as hard as possible, look up and see tears of pain in her eyes, but she doesn't say anything.

"Sorry," I mutter and relax my grip. She smiles weakly. I look at her and know why patients fall in love with their nurses. There is an instant bond, until I close my eyes in pain as the doc decides the tube isn't in far enough.

Back to the surrealistic consciousness of my present experience, struggling back from pethidine induced sleep to a Doctor standing by my bedside. My first impression is his watch, which tells me it's 1545 hrs. He's Australian on secondment and I've seen him a few times with his Boss, that Colonel who seems intent on killing me with his inaction. But this doc is different.

"I'm having you moved to the London Hospital. There's a surgeon there who can take care of you."

"That's quick."

"Nobody knows. I'll get hell for this, but it's what has to be done."

"Will they operate?"

"Probably."

"Will I live?"

"Maybe. He's the best in the world. When you get better you'll want to come back here and hit someone."

Then with a gentle pat on my shoulder he was gone.

When I get better? Is that possible?

I'm still trying to grasp what he said, but everything gets in the way.

Nurses running around.

A gurney slides beside my bed and I'm lifted onto it, and off we go down the corridors, a wild blurry ride, fleeting faces, wobbly wheels, in the distance a siren.

Down the lift and then the warmth of a summer sun as they wheel me to the waiting ambulance.

The orderly is a Para and he lifts me as if I were a baby into the ambulance where a young QA waits to attach my blood transfusion bag to a hook in the roof, along with the feeding bags.

"Shall I use the sirens and lights?" the driver asks the orderly.

"No. He won't make it anyway," comes the reply.

I turn and look at the orderly in outraged disgust.

"Fuck you. I'll make it," I whisper and he has the grace to look embarrassed before the doors close and I'm off on another ambulance ride. How many is that now?

Gazelle helicopter from Crossmaglen to Bessbrook, South Armagh.

Q Car from Bessbrook to Musgrave Park Hospital, Belfast.

Musgrave to Aldergrove airport, Belfast.

Belfast to RAF Brize Norton.

Brize Norton to BMH Millbank, London.

My house in Gluck Strasse, Osnabruck to BMH Munster Germany.

BMH Munster to RAF Gutersloh Airport, Germany.

C130 from RAF Gutersloh to RAF Brize Norton.

RAF Brize Norton to BMH Woolwich, London.

And now BMH Woolwich to the London Hospital.

Where the hell is that anyway?

Is that a real place or are they just going to drive around until I die and then say, *'oh well, he didn't make it. We tried.'*

The QA looks scared shitless, watching me as the ambulance slowly pulls away from the Queen Elizabeth Military Hospital. I try and smile but fail as every bump in the road is an agony and it seems like we're riding over corrugated iron, the vibration unbearable. I wonder just how old she is. Nineteen? Twenty? Who knows? The blood transfusion bag sways on its hook in the roof and as the ambulance bounces over a large bump it jumps off the hook and falls on the floor, the QA scrabbling about trying to pick it up, as the ambulance gathers speed and then brakes hard as the traffic lights up ahead change. Again the image of Tommy Cooper springs to mind and I can't believe this circus.

Perhaps I really am dead and this is the Devil's way of fucking with me before I have to stand on my head in a pile of shit for eternity. If I was really going to Heaven surely God would have planned it a little better.

Nothing makes sense anymore.

Nothing seems real.

But it is.

I know it is because each agonising spasm screws my legs up into my chest so that I'm like a human ball, wound up tight and bleeding from my arse onto the stretcher. The QA steadies the blood bag as it threatens to jump off its hook again.

We both watch it intently as if it's an animate thing with a mind of its own, and we're wondering what it's going to do next. Eventually, knowing she can't do this for the entire journey, she just holds it. What does it matter anyway? They told her I wouldn't make it and she drew the short straw, now she's terrified in case I stop breathing, or my heart gives up, and she has no idea what to do. I don't even think there's a defibrillator on this ambulance.

Time is meaningless to me. I have no idea how long the journey takes as we get caught in traffic and I can see the resignation on the young girl's face. The hopelessness and fear in her eyes.

"Don't worry. I'm not going to die on you," I say and try and smile again, but my voice is barely audible and my smile halfway between a grimace and a scream.

I must have passed out because when I open my eyes, the doors of the ambulance are open and there is a flurry of activity. The QA smiles tentatively in relief and touches my shoulder. There's a lot of that going on, it's like a final gesture, the wave as you pass on to...

To what?

I don't know and I don't care because I'm not passing on to anything, I'm staying right here on Earth. I have a family to go back to and an unborn baby.

Crowded corridors, water pipes, nurses, gurneys, patients, doors banging open and the flicker of passing overhead lights. And a sickly smell of boiling beef somewhere. It's always either beef or cabbage. Yet another mindless meander as the gurney squeaks along the corridor. Another lift and another corridor then strong hands lift me onto a bed. At the end of the bed I see a very dapper man. Smoothed back hair, immaculate dark blue pinstriped suit beautifully tailored. If he had had a moustache I would have thought it was Hercule Poirot.

"Hello Captain Clarke. I am Peter Roberts, Sir Alan's senior registrar."

"Sir Alan?"

"Sir Alan Parks, he's at a Banquet but will be here for the surgery. He'll see you in the Theatre. Just need to check a few things and we'll get you straight up there."

Then, for the first time in nearly a month I relax, because now I know that I'm in the hands of skilled professionals. People who know how to save my life and are not afraid to do what has to be done. People with a quiet confidence in their ability, and I silently thank the Australian doctor.

The nurses prepare me. Peter Roberts does his once over and smiles. "Don't worry. We'll have you right in no time."

But I don't care now.

I'm going to surgery and they are going to put me to sleep like the dog I am, and if I never wake up again at least I will go without pain.

Then it's another gurney and more corridors, another lift and more corridors, but the hurly burly of the ward becomes the efficient silence of the Operating Theatre. They don't take me into the prep room, they wheel me straight into the Theatre, lift me onto the most uncomfortable slab known to man and start shooting anaesthetic into my arm as a very tall man with huge hands leans over me.

"I am Alan Parks. I'll see you when this is all over."

"Count back from one hundred," says another voice.

"Ninety nine... ninety..."

And just before I lose consciousness I see that the tall man is wearing a dinner jacket and black bow tie.

Yes, God is definitely a comedian.

"...eight... ninety seven... ninety..."

Then the lights go out.

0700 hrs. 28th July 1977

In the twilight of dying
There is no peace.
Just my fingernails
Digging into the cliff edge
Of Life

Weird mixed up dream nightmares flood my mind. Manic scenes from Bosch's paintings.

But it's a black and white twenties silent film.

A moving, writhing Hell.

There is a man, a Buddha like man, half naked with round glass bottles on a belt around his waist, each with a light brown rubber tube coming out of the top and into his body. He's smiling and tending to the bottles as if they were a garden. Carefully stroking them as the fluid comes from his body and fills up the bottles. Then he carefully empties the bottles into a larger glass bottle that stands on the floor beside him. And all the while strange satyr-like creatures dance around him. Venus rises from her shell. Naked. Perfect. Smiling. Everyone is smiling but it is Hell.

'Yeah though I walk through the shadow of the valley of death I will fear no evil.'

They are the first words that come into my mind as I drift back from unconsciousness. I am not religious so it makes no sense.

God the comedian again, playing with my mind.

"Good morning my little pretties. Grow for me." It's a woman's voice close by, and when I open my eyes I see I'm lying in bed beside a large window. Standing watering plants is a black nurse. She senses me and turns with a big smile.

"Good morning Captain Clarke. You've come back to us."

Is this part of the nightmare still?

She crosses over to me and takes my pulse, blood pressure and

183

temperature.

'No it's not a nightmare. I survived. I actually survived.'

I try to say something to the nurse, but she shakes her head. "Don't speak. You have a tube down your throat. A nasal gastric catheter."

Then my body starts to wake up. I can't move, but I can see that I have a large bandage stretching from my sternum to just above my pelvic bone and another bandage just below that. The sheet covers my private parts. Coming out of my abdomen are three tubes. One big one and two thinner ones, that disappear over the bed. There is also another tube that snakes beneath the sheet, and I know it is all the way up my dick into my bladder. I still have the PICC line in my left arm and the two feeding lines in my right arm. And stuck on my right lower abdomen, is a big beige coloured plastic leech-like bag with a plastic clip on the end. I know what it is and it's going to be my *'friend'* for the rest of my life.

But it's the tube down my throat that is really bothering me. It makes swallowing a purgatory of a dry rasping gag, like swallowing sandpaper. It's the only real discomfort I feel as there is just tightness around my stomach, so I guess they must have filled me up with pethidine.

Breathing's a bastard, the taste of anaesthetic so strong I feel sick but can't retch because if I do I feel the stitches stretching and pulling and I'm afraid I'll rip open like a haggis at Hogmanay.

That's fine. I can just drift in and out of consciousness now, knowing that I am alive.

Alive.

Three weeks ago I was preparing for death.

Gluck Strasse, Osnabruck, Germany 4th July 1977. It's six in the morning and the bed's wet. Did I just pee myself? Can't be, I've never peed myself not even when I'm blind drunk. No, that's not true. There was this time when I was with the French Paras in Pau and...

But that's another story.

With difficulty I pull back the covers and see I'm lying in a pool of blood. My gut hurts like hell. My wife struggles awake and I ask her to telephone the medical centre for some help. She comes back five minutes later telling me that they told her I should report at 0830 when the MO gets in. I ask her to go down to the medical centre at the end of the road and get them to send an ambulance because I'm haemorrhaging. That's unfair because she's seven and a half months pregnant with our third daughter, but I need to be in hospital and I know it.

Yesterday I finished a ten-mile battle march and felt completely knackered. The pills the MO has been giving me are causing all sorts of problems and my guts are just one constant pain. Jesus what's with that MO? He's completely incompetent. He's the new MO, joined us just before the move to Germany and the man's a menace. Wish Alastair had stayed as our MO. I trusted him. I keep telling the Major, the new MO, that the cellulose tablets aren't doing me any good, neither is the cocktail of other drugs he says I should take, including loperamide an antidiarrhoeal. There's something else too, but I don't know what the hell that is, just know it has been screwing with my mind, causing dizziness, mild hallucinations and frantic episodes that I can only describe as mind altering. The pills are small and white so I figure they must be steroids.

He keeps telling me I'm a Para and should suck-it-up there's nothing wrong with me. Isn't that an American expression? Alastair would have had me admitted to hospital for a full examination, but not this MO who has never even given me a physical examination. Guess he doesn't want to get his hands dirty, too busy playing politics in the Mess and looking up the ladder to a career at MOD.

So apparently the constant bloody diarrhoea isn't an indication that something is terribly wrong. It's been going on sporadically for five months, in fact from about two months after I left the Queen Alexandra Military Hospital

Millbank.

Has he read my medical records?

I've been in two hospitals moron, what the hell do you think is going on?

Now that I'm lying in a pool of blood having haemorrhaged, I know that his treatment has ripped apart my bowel.

Fuck. The IRA couldn't kill me, but the fucking Medical Officer's negligence may well have.

I know I'm dying. I can feel the life oozing out of my arse and the blood continues to seep out of me. How long before that fucking ambulance gets here?

When it finally arrives there is just the driver. Apparently the MO didn't think his presence was required, and obviously doesn't think a nurse or an orderly is necessary.

The driver doesn't like officers and could care less, which doesn't surprise me considering who his boss is, just tells my wife I have to get in the ambulance on my own if I want to go to hospital. So I get dressed in jeans, shirt and slippers, and slowly climb down the stairs to the ambulance. The driver looks pissed off, opens the doors and I lie down on the stretcher. My wife peers in at me as the doors close.

This is surreal. Surely it can't be true and I think I must be hallucinating but I know I'm not. The pain, and the sensation of blood sloshing around in my gut, so similar to when I was on patrol in South Armagh. Jesus, how many times did I have to stop and dive behind a hedgerow to let it all out of me before continuing? Wondering all the time what the Toms must be thinking. They must have guessed something was wrong.

It's nearly thirty miles to the BMH in Munster. Thirty fucking miles, about an hour's drive and all the while I'm trying to hold the blood inside and not shit myself. But it leaks out anyway. The driver's taking the scenic route over every pothole he can find until we arrive, or so it seems. The doors fling open and a middle aged pissed off QA tells me to get out. I tell her I'm in too much pain and 'get a fucking wheelchair' because I outrank her. Once inside an orderly starts to ask for all my personal details. At this point I lose my cool.

"My name is Captain AFN Clarke of the 3rd Battalion the Parachute Regiment, and if you don't get me into a fucking bed and get a fucking doctor now, I'm having your fucking stripes, Corporal."

That shocks everybody. They don't know I am a Captain and a Para, because I'm in jeans and a civvie shirt. And before I know it I'm lying in my own room, between clean crisp sheets that won't be clean for much longer. The rest is a blur as the blood drains from my body until finally a doctor starts a transfusion.

But the bleeding doesn't stop.

When I wake up my wife is by my bed. A friend is babysitting the girls and I don't think I'm going to see my unborn child.

I'm sure I'm dying.

"Take the money and buy a house. Small house, or maybe one of those mobile home things. There'll be enough to buy one for the cash gratuity I'll get on my contract."

A mobile home? Am I nuts? No, it was all I could think of. At least a home that is paid for. I'm trying to think of how to look after my family from beyond the grave. What am I thinking? I'm talking like I'm just going away for a while and I'll be back. But we both know that I'm probably not coming back.

I'm done.

The 29th of July, 1977 is a strange fragmentary blur; without time; without form. I'm just floating along in a semi-conscious cocoon.

And then my heart stops. The medical term is *'the patient was found unresponsive'.*

Pounding on my chest.

Floating sensation as if I'm on the ceiling. I can't see anything, but I can hear urgent shouts; running; a gurney's wobbly wheels vibrating across the floor. Vinyl floor I think. Smooth and glossy. Very clean.

All the while I'm completely free from pain. But something tells me I have to do something, because if I give up and drift away in comfort, it'll all be over.

Everything I've done; suffered; survived will be for nothing. A wasted life. So a part of my mind digs into the cliff edge between life and death and won't let go.

Then the pain comes back again with a roar.

I feel the pounding on my chest.

Open my eyes for a moment and see desperate faces staring down at me.

"We've got him back," I hear someone say. A nurse's voice.

Then nothing.

When I come to I don't know what day it is. Maybe the same day, maybe the next day. I don't know. It's not important. I'm still alive. I know because the tube down my throat is worse than the pain from the surgery. I can't see much because my eyesight is so bad from nearly starving to death. I can't talk because of the tube, I can only look.

Sleep. Wake up. Look. Sleep. Wake up.

Time stretches blankly between shots of pethidine and the interminable *puff puff* of the blood pressure cuff.

When I become conscious enough to be aware of my surroundings, I see they've moved me. Now I'm at the Nurses Station where they can keep an eye on me in case I have another 'episode'.

It's noisy.

Phones ringing. Papers shuffling and the talking. The endless prattle of mindless chatter.

'Did you see Coronation Street last night..... What about Starsky and Hutch....? My boyfriend says he's taking me to Marbella.'

But I don't care because they are the best nurses in the world. They care and they are bright and cheerful and I feel 'at home' here.

They took the tube out of my throat today and decide I have to get out of bed and walk. I'm incredulous. But two nurses grab me, hoist me to my feet and gather up all the drain bags, drips, tubes and everything else and walk me a little way before taking me back to bed and then insist I cough.

"Got to get the anaesthetic out of your lungs. Don't you remember you had to go to theatre again?"

Right. Cough. Hold my gut and hope I don't rip my stitches out. It's painful and all I can manage is a pathetic splutter.

"You'll have to do better than that Captain Clarke."

A gentle reminder that I'm an Army Officer and 'show some backbone'. Isn't that what I said to the Para surgeon who refused to operate? If he could only see me now, back on my way to finding him and smacking him in the face. There's nothing like the thought of revenge to get a good cough going.

"That's it. Well done."

And I flop back exhausted.

More pethidine and those beautiful white fluffy clouds roll over my mind.

I love this stuff.

One shot and I'm drifting away, pain free, gloriously happy and secure in my very own pharmaceutically controlled world. I haven't felt this good since before South Armagh, a lifetime ago.

Thankfully the pethidine keeps the nightmares of patrolling the bomb ridden fields at bay and I drift off to sleep to the *'puff puff'* of the blood pressure cuff inflating, as a nurse checks my vital signs for the thousandth time. It's a comfortingly familiar routine.

In the waking hours I think of my family. My wife nearly nine months pregnant; my two daughters, all so far away in Germany, and hope that my friends and their wives are taking care of them.

I wonder if they know what has happened, whether they know I just died and was brought back again. Whether they really understand the seriousness of this situation.

Just a year ago my career was on the *'fast-track'*, with a glowing confidential report after my tour in South Armagh, warranting a *'Very good'* assessment and recommendation for promotion immediately and Staff College. If you want to be anything other than a passed over Major you have to go to Staff College. Even the Parachute Brigade Commander said I did *'...particularly well in South Armagh,'* and *'I support his recommendation to be a Staff Candidate, and fully endorse his 'Very Good' grading.'*

Now my career is dead. I'm a medical embarrassment.

One of those casualties of Northern Ireland the Generals and the Politicians don't like to talk about. It would be easier if I just died and they could send a 'sorry' letter to my wife and family and shove my file into a dusty box at the back of a warehouse somewhere.

Just another statistic.

Fuck you all. This soldier's not dead yet. I'm coming back. I have a wife and a family and an unborn child.

And that's what keeps me going through all the pain.

But hopelessness is no longer part of my vocabulary. It vanished with my bowel, cremated; vaporised. I have a new beginning and excitement within my soul that I never realised was there. The tough unfeeling person was gone. I didn't care about my career, I was looking beyond to what might be, once I get back on my feet.

It's easy to be optimistic when you're flat on your back surrounded by smiling faces and know that you reached the bottom of the pit and somehow you managed to start crawling back out. It doesn't matter how small that tiny spot of light is to which you are struggling, because it keeps getting bigger, a molecule at a time.

And I think to myself, *'shit all you've got is a bag glued to your side to shit in for the rest of your life. Look on the bright side, you could have lost your legs, or arms, or eyes. You could be deaf, dumb, blind and limbless, but instead you get to stand upright and when people look at you they'll never know.'*

How's that for optimism?

Chris my older brother called the hospital yesterday. And today. Twice. He's giving the nurses a hard time because he wants to talk to me and find out what's happening. He's the only one of my family that's called.

My parents can't, they're in Libya and trying to get through is a nightmare.

Can't understand why my wife hasn't called.

"Your brother's on the line again, Captain Clarke."

The nurse looks across the desk at me, phone dangling in her hand and a resigned expression on her face.

I nod and she comes around the desk to hold the receiver to my ear, as I can't use my arms. Too many needles stuck in them.

"Chris?"

"Hey Tone. What's going on? How're you doin'? What happened?"

The questions come thick and fast in his American twang. Too many years living in California.

"I'm O.K. now," I barely breathe. It's an effort to talk. Takes all my strength.

"What?"

The nurse takes the phone. "He's very weak, he can barely talk, but he's making very good progress." She pauses and rolls her eyes. "Alright then." And hangs up. She looks at me resignedly. "He'll call tomorrow."

Tomorrow. There are so many tomorrows. Every day is a tomorrow and every day a yesterday. All the same drifting in and out of each other in a kaleidoscope of interchangeable events, people, faces, sensations.

"We're casevaccing you to the Queen Elizabeth Woolwich tomorrow," the Doc says, but I'm too tired, too much in pain to care.

Pour blood in one end, out the other.

Another ambulance, this time with a male nurse and sirens and flashing lights as we scream towards RAF Gutersloh. Somewhere along the way a car doesn't hear the siren and slams right into the side of the ambulance, knocking us across the road.

We slither to a halt and the male nurse steadies the drips and transfusion bag. Lots of shouting and another siren as a police car turns up at the scene. My German is not good enough to understand but I get the gist.

The doors open and the cop looks in. Pissed off expression turns to shock as he sees me, then the doors slam shut and we're off again, with a Police escort, sirens wailing. I suppose the Policeman was pissed off because it was another BAOR accident and he's seen too many in his occupied country.

But I don't care.

Drift off to sleep and then sunshine and a stretcher and the smell of AVTUR from a C130 Hercules. Feels like home, but I don't have a parachute this time, and inside instead of four rows of canvas seats, it has two emergency medical units. There's a woman on a stretcher surrounded by a medical team. She's sitting upright, with a tube coming out of the right side of her chest. She smiles. I have my own medical team and a nurse leans over and injects something into my I-V. Must be morphine because those wonderful fluffy clouds take me away as the scream of the four turboprops slide into the back of my consciousness.

When was that? Oh yes, about a week ago. Two ambulance rides ago. Many corridors, nurses and doctors, injections and missed veins, 'popped' veins and *'oh let's try that again.'* Finally just shove a needle into the groin and the femoral vein. Then there was the doctor in the Woolwich who wanted to show off to some young nurses how to screw a tube up the arm and into the top of the heart because the blood wasn't getting through my collapsed veins.

Well, can't complain too much, it worked.

Yesterday, today, tomorrow, all the same.

Memories scrambling for order, among the wildly firing synapses in my brain, trying to make sense of it all.

I think of things randomly, with no specific understanding, or cause. Just think of things as they move me back into the main ward.

Knocking my younger brother off a tree branch by accident and watching him plummet to the ground. We were lucky he didn't kill himself and laughed and teased him because he landed on his head.

The birth of my first daughter in Tripoli, Libya, Neil Armstrong walking on the moon and a revolution all within a month in 1969.

Birth of my second daughter the day I left for Northern Ireland on my first tour in Belfast in 1973. She was over three months old when I saw her next on four days R&R.

Nearly getting killed parachuting when I got entangled and both chutes failed to open, but somehow I managed to get air into mine, and the two of us smashed into the side of a hill on Hankley Common. Me with a broken cheekbone, and the other unfortunate soul with broken legs. He went to the hospital, I went to the Officer's Mess bar and a few stiff drinks before going home.

Idle ramblings of a scrambled mind inside a broken body.

But I'm not angry anymore. I'm happy to be alive and know that I will see my unborn daughter. I will see my other daughters grow up. I will see the next sunrise and the beauty of a summer day. To smell the fresh cut hay and see the clouds of dust from the fields as the combine harvesters grind their way across them.

For seven long years I've been dead. Wrapped up in the Industry of Death, learning how to kill so as not to be killed. Now I want Life.

I want Happiness and Beauty and not Fear and Ugliness.

And then I haemorrhage again.

At first I think I shit myself, but that's not possible anymore, it all goes in the bag.

Ring the bell and a nurse comes running.

She strips the sheet off the bed and I can see that I'm lying in a pool of blood that's just getting bigger. Must be an artery because the blood is pumping rhythmically out of my body.

Somebody shouts for the surgeon, as I grow colder and weaker by the second.

'So this is what it feels like to bleed to death? Not bad. Just drift off as the life-force oozes away.'

Peter Roberts appears and they don't load me on a gurney, instead he shoves his finger up what's left of my arse to stop the bleeding and off we go to the Operating Theatre again, only this time on my bed.

More anaesthetic and then nothing.

It's cold and wet at four in the morning as we slip along the road between the grey houses and sleeping inhabitants of Crossmaglen. A hard wind is blowing the rain horizontally, which helps to muffle whatever noise we make, but my lads are good and there's barely a sound as we squeeze through a hedge and into a field on our way to another OP right on the border. My gut is sore and with every step I feel the blood sloshing around inside me and wonder just how long I can keep going.

It's not bravery, because I'm scared shitless, it's the bond I have with my men. They're my boys. My family here in this hellhole devised by some moronic bureaucratically minded General somewhere in London.

So I owe it to my lads to keep going as long as I can. And all the while I have this feeling that I'm not going back with them. That I won't be there when they breathe a sigh of relief as they sail away from these shores for a brief respite before returning on another tour.

Then the terrain changes from the swampy fields to a bay and it looks a bit like the area around the O'Meath VCP. But we're miles from that aren't we?

Then we're walking through a town again toward a bay.

Then I see a swarm of Paratroopers on a white boat, by a granite quayside.

I thought I was in South Armagh.

No, they are. But where am I?

I know what is real and what isn't. And this isn't real.
There's an old man. A woman. Some kids.
And then a blinding explosion and gunfire.
I don't want this. I don't know what this is.
This isn't my reality.

It stops as I open my eyes. The smell of cordite and co-op mix explosive, also known as ANFO, that fills my nostrils drifts away, as do the sounds of the screams and the sight of shredded bodies spewing their brains and intestines all over me, as the nightmare slowly dissipates to be replaced by the sounds of the ward.

A nurse appears and smiles brightly.

"Your catheter comes out today. You'll be glad about that."

Too right. The embarrassment of having a nurse clean my dick and the catheter is surpassed only by when I get an erection, and the raised eyebrows it causes.

At least I know *that's* working.

Most of the nurses have seen it all before, but this is a teaching hospital and the student nurses get a little flustered. There's damn all I can do about it except close my eyes and pretend I'm unconscious.

But if a little embarrassment is all I have to suffer, who cares?

Of course it's a different matter when they pull that thing out. Jesus, feels like my dick's being scraped clean from the inside and the first pee is a real joy. Feels like pissing needles.

But I don't care. I welcome the pain because I'm alive and there is no description of that feeling of total elation.

Tomorrow they say they're going to take out the drains.

I sleep for a little and then wake to see two of my former fellow officer's in 3 Para standing beside my bed, looking very uncomfortable. They're younger than me and have been assigned to the Depot in Aldershot to train recruits. I wonder if the C.O. sent them because Brigade wants a first hand report. Can't see them making the journey just for the hell of it.

They see my condition and go white as sheets. I was 82 kg of muscle. Now I'm 40 kg of skin and bone. Skeletal. When I talk and try to joke, it's in a whisper.

"What the fuck are you two sorry-looking bastards doing here? Making sure I'm not dead? Do I owe you money?"

They laugh. Sort of. And the weak banter continues for a few minutes before the nurse tells them I need rest. I think they think I'm dying right before their eyes, but they're wrong.

Oh so wrong.

I'll be back to piss off the Generals again.

This should be the best day of our lives. Proud Paras who have just completed the most arduous training in the British Army next to SAS Selection. We started out as 75 recruits on that first day in July 1971, eager to become the best infantry soldiers in the world. Legends from Arnhem to the Rhine; Borneo, Malaya, the Radfan. Assault troops from the sky trained to drop behind enemy lines and secure beachheads in the enemy's defences. This was the final hurrah before deployment to our Battalions as Private soldiers. Our parents are here and we are going to serve them the best meal they've ever had in the NAAFI.

But when we get there, they are lining up behind recruits for cold eggs and bacon, and crap I wouldn't give my Irish Setter.

I lose it and so do a few others. So I hatch a plan, and line up a squad of six men and march to the Officer's Mess.

I want an apology.

When we get there, I knock on the door and wait for an Orderly to appear.

"What the fuck do you want," he says comfortingly.

"To see the Platoon Commander."

"He is having lunch with the General. Can't be disturbed."

"We're not moving until he comes down and talks to us. Tell him Private Clarke is here with a squad."

He sees I'm not kidding and figures it's above his pay grade to argue.

The Platoon Commander and I were at school together. Played rugby, boxed in the school team together, so I figure he'll come and see me, if only to find out what the hell I want.

Ten minutes later and he comes out and stops dead in his tracks. I step forward smartly and salute.

"What's going on Clarke?"

"We won't go on parade unless we get an apology from the C.O. to our parents for the way they've been treated sir."

"What?"

"They were supposed to have a special lunch, sir. But instead they've had to line up behind the recruits for leftovers, Sir."

He's stunned. But he knows me and he knows I'm not lying.

"Okay. I'll look into it."

We don't move.

"I will tell the C.O."

I step back, salute. He's never lied to me either.

Turn, face the squad and march them away.

I smile at the memory. Of course the RSM, 'Nobby' Arnold, wasn't too pleased. Pissed off more like, threatened us with all sorts of dire consequences if we didn't get on parade.

To add insult to injury it was raining, so the parade for all 12 of us was held in the gym. And before it started the C.O. had the grace to apologise to our parents for their treatment. The smiles on our faces as we stood rigidly to attention were difficult to contain. But the smiles soon disappeared as we came off parade and the CSM had me, and a couple of my cohorts, arrested and thrown in jail, threatening us with '*hanging for mutiny*'.

How they ever let me become an officer I'll never know.

The memory makes me snigger, which is the closest thing I get to a laugh and the nurses get concerned because it sounds like I'm seizing again. When I tell them I'm just laughing, or trying to anyway, they sigh with relief and tell me I'd better not do it again.

But laughing is what I do.

Once the drains come out and I have two of the IVs removed I can finally listen to the radio without having a nurse do everything.

Nights are always difficult. Sometimes the pain from the surgery keeps me awake, but I don't want pethidine as the shots in my bum really hurt now and it's black and blue. So I listen to the radio and reruns of the Goon Show. Neddie Seagoon, Major Dennis Bloodnok, Eccles and Bluebottle have me in stitches, so to speak. And the night nurse gets worried at my squeaky sounds until I give her the headphones. Now she won't give them back and it's two in the morning and she's winning the fight because I don't have any strength. Finally, laughingly, she hands back the headphones and, giggling, walks back to her desk and continues to flip the pages of her magazine, looking up occasionally and smiling at me as I continue to laugh without laughing because my wounds hurt.

1000 hrs. August 5th 1978

Hospitals have become
My second home
Nurses
My second family
The smell
My constant nightmare.

This is the day I leave the Army.

Seven years and two months after I began my service here at Depot The Parachute Regiment as a Private soldier, I leave as an officer. I served in Cyprus with UNFICYP; two tours in Northern Ireland; a secondment to the French Paras in Pau and a stint in Germany. My substantive rank of Captain is due to be published today, the day I leave. I have been acting Captain for two years because of my illness, in spite of the recommendation for *'..immediate promotion'* to substantive rank after my last tour in South Armagh in 1976.

I valued my Military service, tried to do my best, gave my large bowel, and much of my small bowel to my country, and have been shuffled out with barely a nod. No ceremony, no fanfare, just a collective sigh of relief from the Generals and the Politicians.

A piece of meat to be sizzled on the barbecue of expedience, and devoured by the incinerator of indifference.

The suggestion was made to me that I simply not renew my contract and quietly say goodbye. Or I could run the Airborne Forces Museum until I retire.

Some choice for a field officer.

'Can I claim disablement?'
'No.'
'Compensation?'
'No.'
'Why?'

199

'Northern Ireland is not a war.'
'You are joking. Right?'
'No.'

A short conversation with my superiors, who simply want me gone. Because as soon as I walk out the door, they can wash their hands of me, and never have to think about me ever again.

Even a letter from my solicitor to the Secretary of State for Defence regarding a War Disability Pension, goes unanswered.

But I don't care at this stage, because I'm still alive.

I guess the final thing that pissed them all off, was that to speed my recovery after the second series of operations earlier in the year, I decided to build a bright blue Beach Buggy with a black hardtop and drive it to work, parking it at the Officer's Mess. Every single day until I left. And that, apparently, was very *un-officer-like*. So the car I drove was important to my career? Oh boy.

Green Converse high-top basketball style sneakers, with bright yellow trim. I stare at them in disbelief as Sandy stands there with a 'what's wrong with these?' look on his face. I can't help but laugh. Jeans, multi-coloured sneakers and a white shirt with dark blue jacket. Great for the King's Road but pretty strange for a Captain in the Army. But I don't give a shit. It's fun and fuck 'em if they can't take a joke.

I had to have shoes because I came to UK from the BMH Munster with nothing, having been casevacced on a stretcher.

Of course it gets more interesting while I'm waiting for the RAF aircraft to take me and service families back to Germany. They're looking at me like I'm from Mars, this skeletal looking fellow with the weird outfit who somebody has announced is a Captain in the Parachute Regiment and is in charge of checking everyone on the flight. Naturally the person most impressed is the General to whom I introduce myself, who would like to brush me away like a piece of dog shit.

But I don't care anymore.

My career is over. I'm a 'bagman' with half my guts missing, who shits into this beige plastic bag attached to my abdomen and whose rectum has been brought out to the front so I have a hole straight through my body, and I'm no use to anybody. Apparently there is a chance they can hook up the rectum to what remains of the gut and I can shit again. Can't see that happening, but at least Sir Alan and his team are optimists.

They call the flight and everybody troops out across the tarmac to the waiting aircraft.

Everyone except me.

I'm walking like a double centenarian, so slowly everybody is already inside the plane and seated by the time I reach the steps. Takes me a few minutes to get up the stairs, one at a very slow time. The cabin is blurry and I'm having a hard time catching my breath but nobody asks if anything's the matter. Even when I tell them I have just been released from hospital. I have an ileostomy bag and an open wound just above my pubic bone where I have to inject steroid foam a few times a day, not to mention suppositories up my arse. Sir Alan is trying to preserve the rectum for any possibility of connecting it up to the small bowel at some point. Until then it's try and act normally.

Nobody gives a shit.

But like the dutiful officer I am, I take a head count and reconcile it to the list I have and then nod to the RAF corporal, who closes the door and I can sit down.

But I don't care.

Fuck everybody.

I'm going home.

The reality is that I really wasn't an *'Officer'* in the way the Army wants its officers. They want cardboard cut-outs that they can manipulate and groom for higher positions. People who will salute and do anything they are told without thinking too much for themselves.

People like me are only useful in war, because we will do whatever it takes to get the job done.

People like me are expendable.

But if we survive then there's a problem because they know that people like me will open our mouths and tell the truth. We won't disclose classified information, we're too loyal for that, but we will tell the truth within the limitations of the Official Secrets Act.

And people like me have done our duty. Suffered for it. And now are being not so gently tossed aside.

But I don't really care too much.

Something fundamental has changed in me and I remember what a friend of mine's mother – who has known me since I was thirteen - said to me when she found out I had joined the army.

'Your not a soldier, you're an artist. A writer.'

And it is that thought that keeps digging into my mind even as I prepare to embark upon a new career. As equally insane as joining the army, but it enables me to recover mentally and be able to manage my disability as best I can.

I've decided I'm going back to motor racing. I'm going to design, build and race my own Formula Ford 1600 single-seater racing cars. The design is already on paper, based upon a Nike FF1600 I bought two years ago, with changes to the chassis and new body design. For months prior to my discharge, while our new house was being built in Thetford, I worked on the design, planned everything and formed a company, *TC Racing Ltd.*

This is going to be my salvation and my family's security. A company that I can build and expand into the future, because the options ahead of me in any other realm of business are not very good, considering my medical status. I think I have a clear vision of the future with my wife and now three daughters, starting anew and looking forward to a new life.

The birth of a child is a remarkable event. And I was witness to my second daughter's birth in 1973, the day I took off for Belfast. There was a problem with my first daughter. A breach birth and the nightmare seems to be happening again.

And my wife and I are back in the BMH Munster and she's in trouble with her labour. The baby is stuck and has been for hours and could die if nothing is done.

"Get the doctor," I tell the midwife.

"I can't disturb him," she says. "He's at dinner in the mess."

"Dinner?" I whisper dangerously, absolutely incensed and my tone is such that she pales. "Get him on the phone and get him up here now."

I may still only weigh about 45kgs but nobody's going to fuck my family around.

They are the reason I survived.

They are my reason for living.

The midwife pauses and then makes the phone call.

The Doc takes his time and saunters up to the labour room as if this is an annoyance. I tell him I'm a Captain too and he'd better do something and fast, otherwise there's going to be trouble, and by that I mean I'll throttle him with my bare hands if anything happens to my wife or child.

When he gets in there he realises that something is badly wrong, kicks me out and proceeds to do what he should have done hours ago.

It seems like an eternity until finally I hear the sound of a baby cry. The sweetest sound anyone can ever hear and I break down and cry, a skeletal Paratrooper crying in an empty corridor. The door opens and I'm let inside. My wife's drugged up to the eyeballs, exhausted, pale and in pain. And there is our daughter, her head bent out of shape by the forceps, the marks clear on her temples, as they manhandled her into this life.

But she's alive.

They're both alive.

Just a week ago I was discharged from the London Hospital. Barely able to walk, too weak to climb stairs without pausing every step as I crawl, but released none-the-less to return to Germany. No fanfare. No driver to take me to Stanstead Airport to catch the flight, just the good heart of a family friend.

But I don't care, because the day the Military Medical Services washed their hands of me, I was on my own. Even though I am still a serving soldier.

Settling into a civilian life is strange and daunting. None of the principles that guided my life in the Army apply. It's a jungle where everybody is out for themselves. Honour, loyalty and trust are simply words bandied around with no meaning. There's nobody out here that would lay down their life for me, even though they talk a good game.

It's a strange world, but at least I have a semblance of health. The last operations were hard, the alternative not acceptable, and it's taking time to get back into shape. I've had revolutionary surgery to form an internal pouch out of the small bowel and evacuate it through my arse, but in order to do that, every time I go to the toilet I have to push a catheter up my arse into the *'pouch'*. Sometimes it gets caught in my gut and gets stuck and it takes time until I can get it loose, get it into the *'pouch'* and let the shit pour. Even with liberal applications of lignocaine anaesthetic gel, it's a tricky and painful procedure. Then I have to carefully pull it out and then wash it through, put it in a plastic bag with the lignocaine gel and stow it in a pocket.

There are only a few who have had the surgery, all guinea pigs, and I was the seventh in the world. And I'm glad that my decision to be a *'guinea pig'* can at least help future ileostomy patients lead a relatively normal life. But the threat of a dangerous bowel blockage remains.

"If you get a blockage," Sir Alan tells me, "you have to get to the

hospital within twenty fours hours."

"Or what," I ask naively.

He looks grim. "Or you will probably die."

Sir Alan is not one to mince words and he wants me to face the harsh realities of my condition. However distasteful it may be to me, I have a disability. I have lost normal function of my bowel and I have to be careful with diet to avoid complications down the road. I will suffer from dehydration; inability to absorb vitamins and minerals properly; inability to absorb iron properly and general inability to receive the full amount of nutrients from food without taking supplements. Many of which can't be absorbed. I have to train my small bowel to do the work of the large bowel.

At twenty-nine years old, I'm not ready to become incapacitated and succumb to the difficulties that most people scorn as an *'an old person's ailment'*. There is tragically little education about colostomies and ileostomies, that people associate only with the elderly, which are in fact suffered by people of all ages. From the very young, to the very old. And knowing this, I offer to help Sir Alan by visiting patients who live in fear of having an ileostomy to save their lives. Who would rather die than 'live with a bag'. It's the least I can do for the man who saved my life.

At least having this *'internal pouch'* means I can wear racing-car seat belts and continue to fly aircraft.

There are three things that I love outside my family.

Flying.

Sailing.

Motor racing.

Not in that order. Equally. I have a passion about all of them, which is why I built the Beach Buggy. It was therapy after my surgeries and helped speed the healing process. Too much time dwelling on the medical problems would have spelled depression and inaction. By concentrating on cars, boats and planes I focused my mind outside my body. Forced it to work as best it could, and that, together with hard exercise, got me back from the dead to where I could at least provide for my family.

Some denounced me for my decisions, derided me for being 'irresponsible', but I've always tried to use whatever abilities I have for my family, however bizarre it may seem from the outside. My body isn't normal anymore so why should I behave in a way other people deem to be 'normal'. What is normal for them is not normal for me, because every hour of every day I have to think about the most basic functions everybody else takes for granted. I have to think about food; shitting; what can cause a blockage; why am I feeling lightheaded; to drink enough electrolytes all day long; vitamins; minerals.

Every hour of every day.

And the only person who knows what's going on is me.

Why?

Because I don't discuss it.

It is what it is. Get on with it.

You're an ex-Para, and what got you through training and selection, will get you through this. Mind Over Matter. It doesn't Mind and I don't Matter.

There's nobody out there to help, except my mother, who is doing everything she can to help me through this and support my family, even though she and my father are still in Libya working for an engineering company.

Strangely it doesn't seem as hard as it really is. I feel free for the first time in my lifetime. It's an illusion of course, but that doesn't matter, because it's real to me and it's what keeps me going. Besides, what's not to be happy about?

My own business.

Designing, building and driving racing cars.

How many people would give an arm and a leg for this?

The pursuit of money has never meant anything to me, because all the money in the world simply cannot buy the experiences I've had. I was born in Hong Kong; lived and went to school in India; lived in Iran, and lived and worked in Libya, leaving the latter after the Revolution in 1969. That was an interesting time and my first introduction to being shot at, by someone trying to kill my younger brother and me. Lucky they were such bad shots.

But all that's behind me now and I am staring at my newly delivered racing car chassis and bodywork. The first Hermes FF1600.

And the doubters said I couldn't design and build a single-seater racing car.

Huh!

Of course test-driving it at over a hundred and forty miles an hour on the track at Snetterton, just down the road from Thetford, is a whole different ball of wax. Just have to make sure everything is bolted up really tight. There was a reason I chose to live here in Norfolk after the army. It was here at Snetterton that I first learned to drive racing cars after coming back from Tripoli Libya at the end of 1969.

My dream had been to learn at the Jim Russell Racing Driver's School, so I enrolled with the idea I might become a Professional Racing Car Driver. After all, Emerson Fittipaldi came here to learn and so did Carlos Pace and others. I did the course, ran some races; won some races and when I was offered a team seat the following year had to turn it down because they wouldn't pay me, just provide the car and I had a wife and daughter to feed and a mortgage to pay. So I remembered John Ridgeway and Chay Blyth crossing the Atlantic in a rowboat and they were Paratroopers. So why don't I join the Parachute Regiment for a few years, put some money away and come back to racing or sailing or whatever when I leave?

The thought of going to war only fleetingly crossed my young naïve mind. After all it was 1971 and Northern Ireland was a problem, but nothing huge. Just a nuisance at this stage. A situation that would change in a flash as Bloody Sunday erupted in 1972 and sparked a real organised uprising.

The ground shook a split second before the blast from the explosion reached our ears. We instinctively know what it is, and race outside, thoughts of lunch gone as we look for the source. Running around the building, as the echo of the explosion drifts away, we can see a cloud of smoke rising from the location of Brigade HQ. Even at five hundred metres away the smell of explosive is strong in the air and we all know what's happened, just not which building. As I run up the road I'm wondering how stupid it is to have an Army Barracks set up like a University campus, with no security to speak of and civilian cars able to drive past the Messes and the Barracks' offices.

I'm here in the Parachute Regiment Depot as a Lance Corporal waiting to go to Mons Officer Cadet School having passed my selection for Officer Training, otherwise I'd be in Belfast or South Armagh. Now Aldershot is on the front line.

There's no doubt it's retaliation for Bloody Sunday, which happened three weeks ago.

But just how bad we don't know.

Sirens scream as fire engines and police cars descend upon the scene. And hoping they don't get too close just in case there's another bomb waiting to go off.

It's surreal.

Bombs in our backyard.

How many dead, wounded, who knows.

It's the Brigade Officer's Mess. And it's an empty smoking shell, with the front windows blown out, trees shredded and clothing and body parts on the ground and in the branches. Survivors have staggered out of the rubble, pale and shocked but otherwise not seriously injured. Some with cuts from flying debris and all unable to hear from the blast.

Soon the scene is awash with medics, soldiers, firemen, policemen, MPs, ambulances and my friends and I are just useless spectators. So we turn away and head back down to the Depot and our duties training recruits.

We feel frustrated, futile anger. The desire to get over there and kill the bastards who did this. Escalate the violence even more and raze the fucking country to the ground. But it is part of Great Britain. They are British and the confusion, sadness and anger deepen.

Nothing getting done today.

This is a sobering reminder of what is happening just across the Irish Sea. Of what happens every single day in Belfast, South Armagh and Derry.

Today the war in Northern Ireland came to our house.

And just as in Derry, killed innocent civilians.

For what?

Just to make a political point?

It's almost never the perpetrators of violence that are killed. It is the innocent who take the blast. The bystanders who just want to live their lives in Peace and take care of their families.

On both sides.

For the two years since leaving the army, even the joy of driving racing cars did not rid me of the bad taste of my tours in Northern Ireland. None of it made any sense and everything I read was tinged with bias, either one side or the other. Those that wrote behind false names, and produced books that glorified the fight against the 'terrorists'. But by far the balance was on the side of those that opposed Irish nationalism, for no other reason than they were ignorant of the history of the 'Plantations' by Protestants to drive out the legitimate landowners.

And it sickened me because so many British soldiers died and were maimed in a War they had not been told the truth about. A War no politician admitted was a War at all, and simply hid behind their rhetoric, false claims and false promises. And the British soldier bore the brunt of their lies and incompetence.

So in the spring of 1980 I decide to write down my own account of what happened during two tours with the Parachute Regiment in Belfast and South Armagh. Not a 'Death or Glory' book, but a book of what really happened. A book of how I felt at the time. An emotional book about the fear, the squalor, the boredom and the violence.

I had time on my hands as my dream of creating a racing car

company died amid the naïveté of business, ignorance and lack of money. Not that my cars were not good, they were. But because I had no idea how to run a business, because I had only been trained in the business of violence. I was ill equipped to enter the world of finance and entrepreneurship. After all, I was a Para struggling with a disability that I constantly denied was a disability. It was a pity, because I really loved driving racing cars. The balance when you get it right and the struggle when it's all wrong. It's a three-dimensional chess game in your head as your mind becomes the car and when it's absolutely perfect, it's the most incredible feeling in the world.

But my dreams of winning the Formula One World Championship die in the dust of shattered dreams as the Bank takes back their loan.

So I sit in the spare bedroom and write every day. I wear my beret, have my notebooks and my memories, my area maps and the constant film playing in my mind. And when I'm done I put the manuscript into a bedside drawer in the spare room and forget about it.

I thought I had cleansed my soul by writing everything down. Everything within the rules of the Official Secrets Act, because I still cared about Honour and Duty. I still believed in England, in Great Britain and the ethics and morality that being British meant. I was naïve and desperately seeking an answer as to why I had been manoeuvred into behaving in a way I never would have believed I could have behaved. I was angry at what had happened to change me from an easygoing happy individual into a violent, unpleasant, hard-as-nails, son-of-a-bitch.

But the responsibility is all mine. I was the one who decided to join the Army and I was the one who wanted to join the Parachute Regiment.

There was nobody else to blame.

And responsibility is what I considered I had avoided, and why I sat down to write CONTACT, as an effort to take responsibility for my thoughts and actions and to tell the truth about how we went about our 'business' as soldiers in Northern Ireland. About the intent of the Government and the Army Commanders to 'teach the hooligans a lesson', and by inserting The Parachute Regiment into no-go areas to break the blockade and assert our dominance in the strongest possible way.

Writing CONTACT was both a purge and a purgatory. Truth has always been important to me and when I haven't been truthful I've always suffered a guilty conscience. So reading books about Northern Ireland I was struck with the manipulation of the Truth to enhance a political or religious, or military agenda. It was then that I realised full force that the old adage, *'Truth is the first casualty of war'*, is the Truth.

Truth and Responsibility are soul mates.

Many officers-in-command of a unit, be it a platoon, a company, a battalion, a brigade, a division or an Army in any given situation never want to take responsibility for their failures, especially if they result in civilian deaths.

It would be career suicide.

The Americans, those great justifiers of everything they do, call it *'collateral damage'*, as if the wounding or deaths of civilians are an acceptable consequence of implementing a political agenda.

Except of course when *your* family, *your* neighbourhood, or *your* city is the *'collateral damage'*.

During my Army service I was in front of a few Generals who didn't like what they saw as conduct prejudicial to good Public Relations. What they meant was, that telling the Truth was not what they wanted to project to the general public.

Image is everything.

And if you have to lie and cheat to preserve an image then have at it.

> *"Tony," the OC of Recruit Company in the Depot says as I stand to attention in his office. "We had a directive from Southern Command to let some TV journalist film what we do, and as your Platoon is in Barracks this week you are the one in the barrel." He smiles and it's not pleasant. "Any interviews, you make sure you're there. Stop it if they ask*

dodgy questions."

"Yes sir," I say, salute and smartly leave the office.

Wonderful, I have to babysit a journalist and a TV camera crew.

When was the last time that happened?

Belfast last year, when ITN News sent TV journalist David Rose to cover the riot and gun battle on the Shankill.

What the hell. Let them film the assault course, interview a couple of the Toms and then we can get back to work. Besides, I'm proud of our Regiment. We're the toughest in the British Army and this will show everyone just how tough we are.

On TV for all to see.

So we do just that.

We drive the recruits over the assault course, pushing them, screaming at them, whacking them on their belt pouches if they falter, pouring abuse to get them to drive themselves over the obstacles, not accepting failure. And all the while the camera rolls.

As far as I'm concerned, it's all good stuff. The reality of our training. Showing just what bastards we are and what we expect our soldiers to be able to endure. War is not easy, but our training should be harder. When the bullets are flying there are no second chances. I know because I've been in a gun battle. I've had to rely on my soldiers when my life was on the line. And this is where it all starts, here at the Depot. Every other unit in the army goes through a centralised basic training, but not here. We are the 16 Independent Parachute Brigade and we have our own basic training; our own Battle School in Sennybridge in the Brecon Beacons in Central Wales; our own No.1 Parachute Training School at Abingdon.

Nobody tells us what to do.

We do it our way.

Ray Gosling and the TV crew seem to enjoy what we are

doing. It's great television and myself, the Platoon Staff and even the Recruits are enjoying it too. The Recruits can point to the film footage and say 'that's what we had to go through. That's what it takes to be a Para'.

If you can maintain your own sense of self, your own identity though all the hard physical exercise and abuse, then you are worthy to become a Parachute Regiment soldier. We don't want 'yes men' *we want tough individuals who will be willing to give their lives for their mates.*

And Aldershot is our town.

Now this is all very well, until the General in charge of Southern Command gets a note from the Ministry of Defence to say they are very displeased with the final cut of the documentary.

"Lieutenant Clarke, have you any idea how you have embarrassed the Army?" the General says, as I stand to attention and inwardly shake my head yet again.

This is the second time I've been in front of the General. The first time was when I was at Mons Officer Cadet School and I had to threaten and beat a 'foreign' *cadet in order to save his life on an exercise across Dartmoor. That is, me and another cadet, Peter, who was also slated to join the Parachute Regiment. It was miserably cold in the middle of the night and we knew he wouldn't survive if he stopped moving, so we terrified him into completing the over-night navigation exercise.*

"No sir," I answer truthfully.

"What on earth did you think you were doing allowing them to film this?"

"It's what we do sir. It's our training. I was told to show them everything."

That really pisses him off. I can almost see the steam coming out of his ears. Because what Ray Gosling filmed was exactly what we did in our training. Everybody knew it. The brass knew it. But apparently it wasn't good PR.

> *Well fuck you General, I'm not a Politician, I'm a Parachute Regiment soldier and this is our training, like it or not.*

Truth.

What does that mean?

I know the meaning of my truth. My truth is what happens daily. It's the guilt I feel for every *'white lie'* I tell and convince myself it's okay because in the long run it just doesn't matter.

But it does.

Truth is what makes us moral human beings.

Truth is what makes sense of our lives.

Everything else is Illusion.

So I write the Truth. I write what we did and how it felt. The fear, the arduous physical activity, the boredom and the insanity. I write the Truth of what we do as well as what the enemy do.

Nobody is innocent.

We all have guilt.

Some more than others.

Three weeks of reliving every moment of the two tours in Northern Ireland.

The incompetence of the commanders; the insanity of our orders, and the surrealism of being an occupation Army on home soil.

So sitting here in Thetford in 1980 trying to make sense of it all, was at best an exercise in futility, and at worst a headlong plummet into an insane world where violence is justified and the death of a friend to be honoured and lauded.

What we do is Right. What the enemy do is Wrong.

But who makes those rules?

The Truth is the only thing that makes sense. The only thing that can take me through the quagmire of guilt and fear.

So I sit and write stream of consciousness style, as everything that ever happened during those two tours pours out, and my spare bedroom becomes a battlefield with the stench of explosives, crack of rifle and submachine gun rounds, and faint smell of stale food;

unwashed bodies and rotting bricks and mortar; shit drifting down the open sewers of Fort Knox on the Crumlin Road in Belfast, and the rain, mud, gruelling patrols and constant fear of South Armagh.

Three weeks later I'm finished, the manuscript is written, a pile of paper sitting on my desk and I burn the patrol logs and notebooks, maps and memories, then slip the manuscript into a bedside drawer of the spare bedroom.

It's done and I don't want to think about the Army and Northern Ireland ever again in my entire life.

The book has been a purgation of the doubts, fears and guilt that have infested my every waking moment since the last tour and I think I can safely hide the manuscript away and forget it ever happened.

"CONTACT. WAIT. OUT."

Photographs

The front cover image is based on the original photograph by Jonathan Olley (shown below) in his photographic essay Castles of Ulster, of the Golf Five Zero observation post erected in Crossmaglen after one of my soldiers, Private James Borucki, was killed by a bicycle bomb on that corner on August 8th 1976. It was known as "The Borucki Sangar" by soldiers who subsequently served in Crossmaglen and manned the post. The photograph is reproduced with Jonathan's permission - www.jonathanolley.com

One Platoon A Company 3PARA – Crossmaglen 1976
(I am standing in the centre. Pte. James Borucki is kneeling far right)

Pte. Mark Dodsworth (standing far right back row) and L.Cpl. Stewart McLaughlin (standing middle row third from the right) were killed in the Falklands conflict on Mount Longdon with 3PARA in 1982.

Before joining the Army I raced cars at the Jim Russell Racing Driver's School in 1970. Here I am on pole with a Lotus 51C and won the race.

After my surgeries in 1977/8 and before leaving the Army I built this Dune Buggy as therapy and had fun on the Aldershot tank tracks.

After leaving the army I designed, built and raced my own Hermes 1600 FF cars professionally. Above full-bore at Brands Hatch in 1979. And below, in the centre front row after the start at Snetterton.

With my Piper Warrior II at Norwich airport and flying to Biggin Hill 1983

TOP-FLIGHT AUTHOR

THETFORD author Tony Clarke has become a director of Norwich Air Training flying school based at Norwich Airport.

Writing as A. F. N. Clarke, the former Parachute Regiment captain is the author of a best-seller, "Contact," which tells the story of a soldier's life in Northern Ireland.

He met Alan Belham.

NAT's managing director and chief flying instructor, when learning to fly over a year ago.

He states that having left the Parachute Regiment in 1978 he was looking for an exciting interest. After a short spell of Formula Ford racing he took up flying.

"I found motor-racing expensive and of no practical use, as compared to flying, which has a definite and lasting application."

He says: "NAT is easily the best flying school I have experienced and after a year spent gaining more advanced qualifications it made sense for Alan and I to team up.

"Our aim is for NAT to expand while maintaining its successful formula of providing friendly but in-depth flight training courses in the best machinery available. We pride ourselves in producing not only good pilots but safe pilots as well."

Pictured with their custom-built flight training aircraft, the Piper Tomahawk, are author Anthony Clarke (left) and chief flying instrucor Alan Belham. Both are directors of Norwich Air Training.

NEPENTHE a 10.7m Columbia our home in the USA for fifteen years with our dog Lucy, my wife Krystyna, and my sister-in-law. And below with my mother who persuaded me to have CONTACT published in 1983 - and to whom this book is dedicated - enjoying a sail in Marina del Rey California in 2000 two months before she died of breast cancer.

1975   2010

Other books by the author

literary fiction
COLLISIONS
AN UNQUIET AMERICAN
DRY TORTUGAS

humour/satire
THE BOOK OF BAKER: *Part One: Dreams from the Death Age*
THE BOOK OF BAKER: *Part Two: Armageddon*

thrillers
THE ORANGE MOON AFFAIR (A Thomas Gunn Thriller)
THE JONAS TRUST DECEPTION (A Thomas Gunn Thriller)

I hope you found this book informative and rewarding and if so I would very much appreciate if you would post a review and a 'like' on my Amazon page. To learn about new releases, special offers and free books please leave your email address on my secure website.

www.afnclarke.com

Field Marshal The Viscount Montgomery*:*

"What manner of men are these who wear the maroon red beret? They are firstly all volunteers, and are then toughened by hard physical training. As a result they have that infectious optimism and that offensive eagerness which comes from physical well being. They have jumped from the air and by doing so have conquered fear. Their duty lies in the van of the battle: they are proud of this honour and have never failed in any task. They have the highest standards in all things, whether it be skill in battle or smartness in the execution of all peace time duties. They have shown themselves to be as tenacious and determined in defence as they are courageous in attack. They are, in fact, men apart - every man an Emperor."